A YEAR IN INK

Volume 6

A YEAR IN INK

SAN DIEGO WRITERS, INK

ANTHOLOGY

Volume 6

EDITED BY MICHAEL KLAM

AND ANTHONY BONDS

THE
INK SPOT
PRESS

San Diego, California

A YEAR IN INK, VOLUME 6 is a publication of
The Ink Spot Press
San Diego Writers, Ink
PO Box 34374
San Diego, CA 92163

Many thanks go to our first readers, who are too numerous to be listed here.
Sumilu Cue deserves special note for her tireless copyediting. *A Year in
Ink, Volume* 6 would not have been possible without the support of Lorine
Honeyman, Jill G. Hall, Judy Reeves, Drusilla Campbell, the City of San
Diego's Commission of Arts and Culture, and a grant from the Merci Fund
at the San Diego Foundation.

Managing editor: Amy Locklin

Cover image:
Tapestry with Village Scene
Africa, Egypt, 20th Century
Wool, 94 in. x 57 1/2 in. (238.7 cm x 146 cm)
Photography by Lynton Gardiner
Image Courtesy of Mingei International Museum

Cover and layout and design: Golden Ratio Design

ISBN: 978-0-9799204-1-7

Printed in the United States of America
Printed by Lightning Source Inc.

Commission for Arts and Culture
City of San Diego

TABLE OF CONTENTS

for L.H.

FOREWORD BY
AMY LOCKLIN

COMMONLY TODAY MANY WRITERS TYPE THEMSELVES via a genre, such as "I'm a fiction person," "I'm a nonfiction person," and perhaps more commonly, "I'm not a poetry person."

A discerning reader will note that the pieces included here are not identified by genre in the table of contents or title pages. Poems may be identified by verse lineation, but prose expands from the popular flash or short-short forms to longer fiction and nonfiction. Poetry in terms of possible form and content ranges as vastly as prose.

A discerning reader will also discover that many authors included in this volume of *A Year in Ink* write in multiple genres. San Diego Writers, Ink, supports the idea that writing in all forms can lead to better writing in any form. As one of our screenwriting instructors mentioned recently, poetry for screenwriters is like ballet for football players.

Though arguably achieving a renaissance in literary and performance forms, poetry seems to me to live in the most popular form of contemporary writing: advertising. Think of poetry's use of metaphor and association, compression, economy, and play. That kind of writing can only be achieved through a careful process of revision. As you may guess, San Diego Writers, Ink, also supports the idea of writing through phases of development and improvement.

Because *A Year in Ink* uses anonymous selection in the manner of most contests, chosen work strives toward these ideals. In addition, authors published for the first time have as much chance as seasoned veterans. I thank our poetry and prose editors for their hard work making selections and hope you will too. Enjoy!

–Executive Director, SDWI

INTRODUCTION BY
MICHAEL KLAM

I'VE PERFORMED, HOSTED EVENTS, AND TAUGHT POETRY in San Diego for about 15 years. I've noticed that when most writers start out, they need someone to help keep them busy. Sit down and write! Get up there and read! When it's just YOU at home ("mwah ha ha, let's get drunk and eat chocolates") telling yourself to start typing, things either shape up and flow or turn sloppy.

Boffed by the muse, you might get lucky in your sloppiness and write something ingenious, but generally, crafting a poem is an ordeal. It's work, a labor of grunting and dissatisfaction. There are the magic moments, don't get me wrong, but even the greatest of the greats turned gray perfecting the lines.

One of my younger students came to me recently and said he couldn't write today because his pencil was tired. At least three of my multiple teacher personalities shot up to respond. "Get back to work," thought the first teacher who has heard it all before. "Hey, nice metaphor, now get back to work," thought the second teacher who has heard it all before but still cares. And then third teacher who loves to be on vacation almost said, "Here, here young Frodo. Let's skip the writing and go kill some beasts, live it up instead of scratching the paper with those dreary pencils."

First and second teachers won out, of course, and the kid ended up writing a fabulous poem comparing his life to a Cyclops beating the earth with hungry fists.

And that's mostly it. Get started. Do it and see what happens.

I tell my students to be poets and artists no matter what they become in life. There will be rules everywhere they go, prohibitions, but their inner poet—that slick and wild mastermind of all that is yours and can't be taken away—will not and cannot, by its stony nature, ever be controlled or conquered. Like hope and love and other fantastic thingies that drive us mad while giving us a reason for living, poetry fucking rules.

I tell them to use expletives as little as possible. And to never fear a thesaurus. But mostly I tell them that they've got to do it. Sit down and write. The world is your internet (or is it oyster?).

In choosing poems for *A Year In Ink, Volume 6*, I looked at craft (from punctuation to line breaks to flow), and I considered the time it must have taken to fine tune the piece. I also read each piece to rediscover why I love the genre in the first place. I read to connect, to feel something genuine from one poet to another. I read and reread narratives that made me laugh. I sang the songs and the sonnets out loud.

There is no doubt that every poet who submitted deserves a celebration. I am thankful to have had the opportunity to read every one of the poems.

Alas, there can only be a handful of poems that make it into the anthology. I salute you all and hope to see you in the future on stage and in print. Keep writing.

–Poetry Editor 2012

INTRODUCTION BY
ANTHONY BONDS

M Y CHIEF AIM WITH THIS YEAR'S volume of *A Year in Ink* is that it be a faithful representation of the freshest and the very best work being created by the San Diego writing community today.

The selections in this anthology illustrate the wide breadth of styles San Diego prose writers have to offer. From experimental fiction to realism, from heartfelt mother-daughter story to gritty noir in the pulp tradition, you'll find a vast array of genres in this volume—and irrefutable proof that there are as many ways to tell a story as there are storytellers. As prose editor, I took particular joy in getting to know the extent of our writing community's daring in exploring the exciting, the strange, and the taboo. Diverse though these stories may seem, there is an underlying motif of discovery that binds them together—discovery of the self, and discovery of the potential that lies within others.

David Foster Wallace said fiction's about what it is to be a human being. Selecting pieces for an anthology isn't easy business, and after sifting through many lively, imaginative, heart-breaking, and hilarious submissions, I found that the stories that stuck with me the most were the ones that showed me something about what it means to be a human being.

If I had to put my finger on a theme for the prose pieces that appear in this anthology, I'd say it is this: humanity. Human beings are infinitely complicated and rich with contradiction. In life, perhaps it is a tragedy that an individual is never fully knowable. But in fiction (and non-fiction), this fact is an essential part of what makes a character so deliciously compelling, and is why some characters haunt our hearts long after their stories are over. Honest and true-to-life characters surprise us—and themselves. Some of the most memorable literary characters are the ones that continue to reveal themselves to us at different phases of our own lives. The characters that live between the covers of this collection will, I hope, delight you as they discover strengths they never knew they had, learn something unexpected about a friend they thought they knew, or rediscover hopes they had long since put away.

We tell stories to experience empathy, closeness, and community. Storytelling is something humans have hungered for since stories were first drawn on cave walls. I can't think of a better way to celebrate and strengthen the bond between writers in the San Diego community than by showcasing their stories and poems alongside each other. Experiencing a good story takes a reader out of her natural body and places her in the sensibility of another person. And whether that new sensibility is strange or familiar, we find very often something of ourselves in there inside the heads of others.

As a community of writers and readers, we all have stories to share. Again, to paraphrase David Foster Wallace, we feel a little less alone when our own stories intersect with those of others. Whether you are from San Diego or not, I invite you to explore the pages of this volume, and hopefully find something of yourself.

–Prose Editor 2012

A YEAR IN INK

SAN DIEGO WRITERS, INK
ANTHOLOGY
Volume 6

THE QUESTION

Scott Barbour

JACOB WORE HIS BLUE HOODED SWEATSHIRT like a cloaking device. The hood was always up, except in class or at the dinner table. Sometimes he pulled it far over his head like a monk's hood, until he felt like he was gazing out at the world from the back of a deep cave. Other times he cinched the string so only his eyes were exposed. He stretched the sleeves so they covered his wrists, then poked his thumbs through holes in the wristbands to keep them in place. The front pockets sagged like kangaroo pouches from the pressure of his concealed fists.

After a couple weeks, the sweatshirt started to smell sour—a mixture of unwashed hair and boiled cabbage—and it grew baggy at the elbows, and spotted with grease from microwave pizzas and *carne asada* burritos, and it got more and more comfortable.

"Why don't you wash that thing?" Samantha asked him.

He shrugged and pulled the hood farther over his face.

Despite the smell, she didn't stand farther away.

Under the sweatshirt, he wore two T-shirts—a long-sleeved one with a short-sleeved one on top of it, layered like a mummy in soft cotton material. He wrapped a bunch of hemp bracelets—earthy red and fleshy brown—around each wrist.

He found an old pair of headphones that fit completely over his ears like padded abalone shells. He wore them constantly, unless a teacher or parent made him take them off. Then they hung around his neck, where he liked the way they felt resting against his collarbones. When he put them on and cranked his Rancid or his Rage, he felt safely sealed off—especially with his hood on.

And a book in front of his face.

The book turned out to be crucial. It didn't really matter what book—a fantasy novel, sci-fi, even the latest English assignment—anything to hide his face. But he preferred manga-illustrated stories of teenage ninjas with magic powers and complex personal lives, young men whose fathers had abandoned them to battle the demons on their own.

Equipped this way, with his hood pulled over his head, his headphones over his ears, and a book covering his face, he could float across campus and pass through crowds like a ghost. If you can't hear them call your name, you don't have to talk to them. If you can't be seen, you don't exist.

Samantha was the only one who tried to get through. In trig she complimented his headphones. "Kickass ear goggles."

In art she praised his drawing. "Sick negative space."

He tried to ignore her, but there she was, walking next to him between classes, saying Panic at the Disco and The Academy Is and My Chemical Romance. Saying The Used and Taking Back Sunday.

Soon he said things back to her. Tool. Deftones. Soundgarden.

It was a month before he took off the sweatshirt. Spring came and her bedroom was warm. The third time, he peeled back the sleeve of his long-sleeved T-shirt, but only when she was safely across the room.

When he finally raised his arms and let her peel off the last layers, he had to turn away and let his hair fall across his face.

Later, as they lay together on her bed, she held his wrists, wiggled her thumbs under his bracelets and gently rubbed the red ridges of flesh.

He waited for the question that always came—the one he could never answer, the one that made him shrug and turn away and pull his hood over his head. The few times he'd tried to answer, the words hadn't come. "It was like . . .," he'd started. "I just . . ."

At first he thought it was because of shame, embarrassment. But gradually he realized it wasn't his fault. The question came from people who'd never felt a spring breeze rip a hole in their chest, who'd never felt their blood turn to lead pulling them to the ground. Who'd never had a brain that turned demonic.

Now, with Samantha by his side, Jacob waited for the question, but it didn't come. He closed his eyes and felt her fingers on his wrists, her thumbs massaging the partially numb scar tissue. He heard the quiet, steady sound of her breathing and felt her eyes on him, asking not for an answer but for something else, something beyond words and rational explanations, something even more terrifying to surrender.

MIRROR, MIRROR

Regina Morin

You won't believe this,
but an old woman emerged
from beneath my jeans
just as I dropped trou there
in the hydrogen explosion lighting
of the T.J. Maxx dressing room.
She seemed to have no bones—
only flesh as rippled
as an avalanche of clay.
Those legs could not be mine:
my thighs could not be
so formless and drained of all juice.
Surely the mirror there
performs a transformation,
robbing each unsuspecting
woman of muscle tone and
grace and instead replaces
her stunning thighs and legs
with a hologram of hagdom
that I can't believe emerged
there in the dresing room
at T.J. Maxx.

GROWING UP AND LOOKING BACK

Rebecca Chamaa

I think of you all the time
As the clock ticks
And calendar moves
From week to week
Month to month
Year to year
How did we go from adolescence
To middle age so swiftly
Me in my pink pointed
Tennis shoes with safety pins
Pushed through
Punk rockers
It all seems so tame now
But then it was radical
Racy and anti-establishment
And who is established now
Both of us
Owning homes
Paying our taxes
Paying our dues
Do you ever wish you could go back
To where music and anti-fashion
Were all that mattered
Making a statement
With the color of our hair

or thrift store chic
worn out clothes
I think of you all the time
As I rummage through
Second hand stores
Searching for a step
back to the history
of me

8:00 PM:
BETTY CROCKER'S KITCHEN

Kathi Hansen

A T FIRST CERTAIN THAT SHE'D SIMPLY forgotten to set the oven timer, Betty Crocker, ever the optimist, peers again into the oven at the identical twin cakes, stubbornly shrunken and sulking in their polished pans. Those babies aren't going to rise one more millimeter, she finally concedes, extracting them with monogrammed hot pads from the professional grade, perfectly calibrated (she did weekly checks with an oven thermometer) O'Keefe and Merritt oven, gently sniffing the wafting vanilla perfume up her slender nostrils. It being far too wasteful in both time invested and ingredients consumed (that Madagascar vanilla bean is precious!) to feed to either the garbage or her finicky kids, Betty Crocker sets the little disappointments on shiny racks to cool while she considers her options. Having skirted their destiny as the fluffy foundations for lightly sweetened whipped cream and fresh-from-the-garden spring strawberries, what should become of them now?

As she sinks into her chair at the kitchen table, the metal trim ringing the Formica snags her sheer stocking and draws blood, a sure sign that Roger's Honey Do List needs refreshing. The run tickles up her thigh to its final resting place perilously close to the garter clip under her pleated skirt. Run is right, she thinks, and how funny that a tiny hole could beat a path that quickly north, to territory her husband no longer rushed to explore. Intending to salvage dessert by finding the perfect recipe centered around under-risen cakes, she flips through the tidy three-ring binder labeled "BC's Favorites," sorry that she'd dumped her old over-stuffed, dilapidated recipe box in a daunting and nearly overwhelming effort to please her sullen sixteen-year-old daughter, who gave her the minimally decorated binder—an art class assignment—for Mother's Day. That box may have looked a mess, but Betty Crocker knew its contents intimately—far better than the uber-organized notebook displayed in front of her that she now mightily resents. The oven timer suddenly trills an annoying distraction. No longer the intended reminder that the homemade batter had successfully transformed to golden cakes, the noise now reminds her that it's after eight, the cakes are flat, and there's still no sign of Roger.

In her haste to quell the intruding buzz, she bumps the stack of glossy photos from the table, and the still life impressions from yesterday's photo shoot spill across the shiny linoleum floor. Buttermilk biscuits rising to even the-freshest-baking-powder-on-the-market defying heights. A thick slice, atop a cut-crystal plate, of a four-layer German chocolate cake proudly oozing thick, gooey, coconut butter pecan frosting. Betty Crocker taps a cigarette out of the pack she'd hidden under the kitchen sink and considers lighting it right then and there, impervious to the lingering scent that would raise the suspicions of any of her now noticeably absent family members who might stroll in any second. Instead she steps onto the back porch, extinguishes the porch light, and strikes a match on the redwood rail. As the red glow from the cigarette sends secret Morse Code-like messages to the nocturnal creatures lurking in the oaks, she momentarily revels in the recollection of the burly photographer's surprising appreciation of not only the perfectly smooth consistency (not to mention the exquisite marriage of sweet and tang) of the Meyer lemon curd she'd layered over flaky crust, but the glossiness of the meringue peaking in glorious mounds atop it, as well. He'd gone on about it, his mouth full of surreptitiously stolen bites and his eyes lustful, for hours. Roger, equally brawny (and better looking, really), never notices the out-of-this-world results of her efforts. He'd failed to notice her puffy bruised lips and the purple mark on her neck when he'd come home not long after the photographer had left last night, either. Why hadn't he called to say he'd be late anyway?

Back to scrutinizing the cowering orbs she'd produced, Betty Crocker suffers yet another of her many "what would Sara Lee do?" moments. Friends since culinary school, she knows that Sara Lee's husband came home when expected and that Sara had never been obliged to distract herself from his absence with after-hours, impromptu baking—or lip-locking grunting photographers for whom she'd never grant the time of day under ordinary circumstances. Even so, Sara Lee, if forced to face the depressing music of squat, demoralizing cakes, would most certainly create a lovely dessert from the failed pastries—and pull it off as though that was the original intention all along. Why, at this very moment Sara and her husband were probably fireside, hand-feeding each other jam-filled confections, shamelessly teasing each other about the nether regions upon which they should smear the delicious concoction. Of course Sara and Harry Lee could indulge in such lovely wickedness. They, footloose and childless, needn't ever worry about which of their teenage brood might come charging through the bedroom door at the most awkward moment—or worse—fail to come charging through the front door anywhere close to curfew, a term now as meaningless as marital fidelity.

And then there's this: it's pushing 9:00 PM and Sara Lee's husband is home. Betty Crocker's is not.

One Dish at a Time

Regina Morin

I have read, I tell my husband,
that one no longer needs to
rinse the dishes before loading
the automatic dishwasher.
I tell him that our modern
dishwashing powder seeks out
bits of food on our green china plates,
the better to devour with its
powerful enzyme
the blush of marina, the
haughty speck of blackened toast.
It doesn't matter.
He stands at the sink
with a plastic scrubber in hand
and swirls away each solitude of crumb,
each tiny memorial of egg.

In a thousand, thousand years, no one
will figure out how to make a marriage
last unless we allow one to rinse
before loading the dishwasher
while the other one
says, "I'll let the enzymes do it."

CATHY

Kelly Metz-Matthews

THERE IS A PAINTING IN WHICH I see myself. Almost without warning, this painting managed to weasel its way under the shirt collar of my soul. And it dug in deep. This is surprising to me because I've never had a particularly deep connection to art. Like most, I buy artwork to line the walls of my home and visit museums on vacation so as to not appear completely uncultured. I simply seem to be missing the "art gene" that some have, the one that gives perfectly unassuming people an innate sense of form, line, and color. I either like the look of something or I don't. Perhaps I'm just rather unsophisticated. But it doesn't matter, I suppose, because I do connect with this one piece. An oil on canvas by Bruce Adams, it is called *Cathy*.

Cathy is a nude piece, all soft lines, thick brush strokes, and blending hues. The subject, presumably Cathy herself, has smiling eyes and long red hair that falls in sinewy waves down her shoulders. She has a gently curving belly, rounded hips, and wide nipples barely beginning to slack. She takes up most of the canvas, and yet her presence manages not to overwhelm. She is beautiful, yet flawed. Neither young, nor old. Neither thick, nor thin. Neither vibrant, nor subdued. Instead, she is some amalgamation of these things. When I look at Cathy, I think mostly that she is a woman, that she is all women.

But it is not the authenticity of her womanhood that speaks to me on the deepest level, it is the fact that her body, sprawled softly across a rugged brown duvet, is decorated in tattoos. I see my reflection in that ink, in the act of inking oneself, of branding one's memories, desires, and imagination on one's body—on one's soul, if you must really know. The actual meaning of her tattoos is of little consequence to me; my connection to her is a simple result of our shared experience as women with tattoos, as women who have placed meaning on tattoos. Like Cathy, I know what it is like to be judged by them, to be defined by them. I know what it is like to cherish them, to be empowered by them.

Cathy is, perhaps, braver than me. Her tattoos span various body parts, visible in multiple variations of clothing. I have only one tattoo and although it takes up a large expanse of my upper back, it can be covered should I desire to cover it. Occasionally, people see my tattoo peeking out from under the collar of my boring black button-down and are surprised. Surprised because I don't seem like "the type." Secretly, I like this reaction. There is the predictable: "You got a tattoo?" Other times, the more cringe-worthy: "I can't believe you did that to yourself." Once, my darling grandmother, whom I had not told about my tattoo, came up behind me while I was pulling my long red hair—yes, like Cathy's—into a chignon. Quite suddenly, I felt the air freeze at my back. "Oh my God! You've ruined yourself!"

Have I ruined myself? Has Cathy? I contemplate this. Is ruination not somewhat subjective? Maybe society deems what is "ruined" and they've tapped me on the shoulder: "To the showers with you!" Maybe I ruined myself when I let that Turkish boy take my virginity (in fairness, I threw it at him), or when I smoked pot for the first time. Maybe I ruined myself the first time I dyed my blond hair red, vainly had my doctor inject saline into the little spider veins of my legs, slept with a woman for the first time, or wore something from Forever 21 when I was assuredly forever twenty-nine plus. Maybe. Maybe. Maybe.

Maybe, every time we cover, alter, or transform some nubile part of ourselves, we crush some lingering innocence within us. Or, then again, maybe not. Maybe the thing that one person views as tarnished is, in fact, reborn. Maybe it, through alteration, becomes something new. It is ruined; in fact, it is crushed. But, phoenix-like, it is reborn from its own ashes. I wonder, always, what Cathy would think.

Recently, I was sitting on the floor playing "lions and dinosaurs" with my children. It's our thing. It was humid out, and sweat dripped lazily down the nape of my neck. I had tucked my tank top up over my midriff and between my breasts, hooking it through my bra. My son, the blood-thirsty *Tyrannosaurus rex* of our seated ensemble, came up behind me. Like that day with my grandmother, I felt the air freeze at my back. Then, ever so slowly, I felt the tingle of small fingers along my upper spine. "Mommy," my son asked, "Who drawed this picture on you? Can I draw one on you, too?"

My son didn't see ruined skin that day. He saw a picture, a painting. A *Cathy*. One day, I'll explain to him that mommy got her tattoo for him and for his sister. I'll show him that their names and birthdates are penned inside an unfurling scroll. I'll explain that the mass of flowers surrounding the scroll are blue in honor of their uncle, a man they will never meet, a man who died before they were even a spark of an idea. I'll tell them, in that reassuring way one speaks to young children, that mommy surrounded them with their uncle's favorite color because he is their guardian angel, because he watches over them, protects them.

What I won't tell them, because they are too young and because, at least for now, it is my secret to keep, is that there is a small, nearly imperceptible crack running through the scroll inked into my back. It splits the scroll in half right between their names. For anyone who looks closely at it, this crack appears to be part of the design, simple artistic license on the part of my tattoo artist. But I know otherwise. I know that this crack marks the loss of their sibling, a sibling whose heart stopped beating in their mother's belly. Maybe I'll tell them about their sister one day. Maybe I won't. Maybe I'll keep her for myself. When I look at Cathy, exposed on that brown duvet, I think of myself on an operating table, having a lifeless child removed from my womb. I wonder what secrets Cathy's tattoos are keeping.

Occasionally, I think of my grandmother's comment. I think of it particularly as it relates to my children. They do not see me as ruined. As young children so often do, they think of their mother as a God-like entity. This will, of course, change. Eventually, I will embarrass them, ruin their teenage lives, make them hate me. I can hear it now: "Gosh, mom, I can't believe you did that!" And I will do *that*—whatever terribly punitive thing that is—all for the immensity of my love of them, so that one day, when they grow up, they'll come back to their mother of their own free will.

Who knows what my tattoo will look like by then—ten, twenty, thirty years from now. Cathy was painted in 1998. She didn't look much younger then than I do now. How old would that make her today? Forty? What will my tattoo look like when I'm forty, fifty, older? My skin still snaps back to attention these days; I am only 32. I am not so naïve as to think it always will. Age is a race we do not win.

But, really, that is of little consequence. I've come to see my tattoo as being representative of change in the larger sense. I believe change does erase some of our former selves, but sometimes the residue of change stays hidden away within us, tucked into the deepest recesses of our souls. It stays because it is still part of us; it hides because if we were to access it, it might rise up and take flight. A phoenix.

I know Cathy has dug into my soul because her tattoos preoccupy me as much as my own. I wonder: Does she have more tattoos now, all these years later? Is there meaning behind them? Or, am I naïve to assume that every tattoo is meaningful to every woman? Surely, I must realize that tattoos can be purely decorative. Sometimes, they are little more than tequila-fueled mistakes. Yes, I do know this. But when I look into Cathy's big brown eyes, I feel we are kindred spirits. I choose to believe that her tattoos hold some profound meaning for her, and that our tattoos thusly connect us more deeply.

I see my tattoo as a cocoon, as a place of transformation. It is both the person I was before my brother's death and after. It is the person I was before the loss of my little girl and after. It is me as a woman, carefree and unattached, and me as a mother, a giver of life. It is my link between the then and the now. It is not the phoenix, but the ash, not the caterpillar or the butterfly, but the cocoon that enables its transformation.

I suppose some butterflies throw off their cocoons at birth, as if to say: "Be gone, wretched thing! I am all new!" They see their cocoons as relics, anachronistic reminders of some other, earlier life. But I shall keep mine tied firmly at my back. I am quite proud of it. I will watch as it inevitably shrivels and fades. Like Cathy's will, like they all will. Like we all will. Some will see me as ruined by then, ravaged by the tumults of age. But I am ahead of them in this, for I will have my cocoon at the ready. When it is my time, I shall tuck inside of it, turn to ash, and be reborn.

ONE OF MY ELECTRONS IS MISSING

Regina Morin

"Free radicals are molecules that have lost an electron."
–David B. Agus, M.D.
THE END OF ILLNESS

Once, I lost a pair of sunglasses,
the ones with CK on the temple.
They made me look mysterious
and slightly insatiable.
And the silver bracelet with the
Navajo turquoise blazing inside
its dimpled cabochon, dropped
from my wrist into the deli case
at Maven's Kosher Cafe. Gone.

But now I read that one of
my electrons is missing.
It is rocketing around my aging
frame like a nursery school tot
around the mulberry bush.
It is creating oxidation;
a flame my knee detects
as I rise from bed each day.

Free radicals can kill bacteria
or they can linger in my brain
until the words *free* and *radical*
are placed in the waste bin
along with the names of
my husband or my friend.

They are searching for just one thing:
an electron.
Like the shy girl who waits
at the edge of the dance floor
with the word *Hope* pinned
to her anxious breast,
they are keeping alive the message
that someday their electron
will arrive and lead them
onto the dance floor where they can
twirl and dip their partner in
an eternal dance of life.

The Mechanic

Kate Currer

M Y FAMILY WAS ALWAYS A CAR FAMILY. Take the number of licensed drivers at any given time, add two, and that's how many cars were in our driveway. Less certain was the number actually running. See, my Dad is a mechanic. By hobby, not by trade. When he was fifteen, he and his dad took apart and reassembled the engine of an old Chevy, and he has felt like an expert ever since. He takes great joy in being alone with a machine, tinkering until he thinks he has found the problem. His downfall is that he does not know when to quit, or when to start working on the right thing.

In my dad's mind, taking care of cars was a way to take care of the family. Only, he interacted with machines the same way he interacted with us: in spurts. He could go years without changing the oil in the cars that were working, in the same way he never made it to dinners, basketball games, or plays, or knew the names of our teachers, best friends, or stuffed animals.

Then, in a burst of enthusiasm, he would decide to get involved. My fourth grade science project was to attach a tiny motor to a battery. My dad picked up the components, took them into the garage to "check on something," and emerged with a finished motor and a big grin on his face. My dad helped me cheat, which I had to tell him was wrong and that he couldn't help me with school anymore.

He taught me how to play chess, and we played a few games over a few days. But he never let me win. And then he would gloat over his victories. In frustration, I flipped the board off the table and vowed never to play again.

I had a habit of putting on shows in my living room and hand delivering invitations to my family. I brought one to my dad, working on a car in the garage, and he told me he wouldn't be able to make it. I ripped it up and never invited him to another one. I came to learn that any involvement from my dad would be frustrating, disappointing, or both.

It was the same way when he tried to fix one of our cars. He would only do the work himself, and he would only buy the kind of vehicles that need repairs in the first place. He would start out trying to fix the problem. Then before you know it, Mom has gone six weeks without a car, and I have to ride my bike to school. We drove around with garbage bags for windows, engines that couldn't handle steep hills in the summer, and a constant sense of fear. One Saturday, the whole family was going to drive to the beach together. My dad decided to "check on something" with the car before we all set off. My dad spent the day in the garage, with the car up on a tire jack. The rest of the family spent the day inside, held hostage by my dad's attempt at fixing something.

When I turned sixteen, my sister gave me her car, a 1992 Chevy Cavalier, white with a red racing stripe. It was called *White Lightning*. She got it from her friend who got it from his grandparents. It was like dating an old friend, after you'd met all his ex-girlfriends. It was safe. It was reliable. And my dad never laid a hand on it, partly because I was adept at keeping him away and partly because the car ran perfectly.

Four years later, I was driving on La Jolla Village Drive, and the car stopped driving. It was as if *White Lightning* had muscles, and they all seized at the same time. I pulled to the side of the road, and I found myself in an unfamiliar situation. I had never had a car break down on me before. I called my Mom, but she didn't pick up. So, without thinking, I called my dad. He calmly explained that I should call AAA, have them take it to a mechanic, and that was all I could do.

That was all I could do; that wasn't all he could do. The prognosis from the mechanic in San Diego was that the car's computer had malfunctioned, but he was unable to recreate the misfire. My father, of course, found this unsatisfactory. He bought the professional manual to the car, called from San Francisco to quiz the mechanic about possible solutions, and researched possible electric surges in San Diego at the time of my break down.

When I picked up the car, the mechanic gently asked me, "Did you give your Dad this number?"

"Yeah. I know. I'm sorry."

I somehow kept from telling this mechanic everything. "Look, this isn't the first time he's intruded, it isn't the first time he's embarrassed me, and it certainly isn't the first time he's gotten in the way of something I can handle myself. He may have talked a good game about how much he cares about his daughter's safety, but I know what this really is, and it isn't about me anymore. It's about the car." The mechanic didn't need to hear all that.

A month later, my car broke down again. My only thought was, "I'm done."

When I talked to my dad about getting rid of the car, he was obsessed with the idea of "saving" it. "That mechanic sounds like he doesn't know what he's doing, but I have been reading up in this mechanic's manual, and I have a few ideas about how to save your car he probably didn't think of."

My dad arranged to have my inoperable 1992 Chevy Cavalier towed from San Diego to San Francisco. I stood out in the street as *White Lightning* was placed on the tow truck, alongside a BMW needing expert body work. I was embarrassed. All this money spent on a car that would probably never run again.

That day left me without a car in San Diego, and I spent the next six weeks riding my bike to school.

My dad, like always, focused on the battle in the garage. He would go to Mulligan's Auto Parts, buy one of about 100 connectors that went from the computer to the main engine, install it, then drive until the car broke down on him. Then he would buy the next connector, install it, and await the next breakdown. I felt strange visiting home and seeing my old car being worked apart. It was like my first love was now a heroine addict, still living back in my hometown. I felt so sad to see what it had become, but so glad I got out when I did.

"Dad, you know that even if you fix it, I won't drive it, right?"

"That's fine, I'll just keep driving it myself."

"You know, you're probably spending more time, money, and energy than it's even worth at this point."

He sighed, "I know. But it's not about that anymore. It's about fixing it."

•

For the first time, I really saw my father. I could have been so angry in that moment, all this misdirected energy spent on connections in a car that no one in his family would drive. But I saw the man he wanted to be—someone who fixes things. He just never figured out which things need to be fixed and which things to be left alone.

NEIGHBOR

Eber Lambert

WHEN I WAS A KID WE lived next door to Nikita Khrushchev. Some people may still be surprised to learn that the Soviet Premier lived in a 3-bedroom suburban tract home in Santa Ana during the height of the cold war 60s. At the time nobody knew who he actually was except a few of the neighbors. He lived alone, always waved to folks when he came out to pick up the morning Pravda, and generally kept to himself. His front yard was well-maintained: tasteful, but far from bourgeois. The backyard was a completely different story: large, uneven concrete slabs surrounded by lifeless gravel and cracked block walls. Occasionally he'd have friends over for a BBQ. They'd sit on the rusting steel benches playing balalaikas and singing Woody Guthrie songs late into the night until Mr. Birch in the house on the other side would yell over the fence that he was calling the cops.

Sometimes my friend Charlie and I would hang out in his garage with him. We called him Kroozie. Always wearing the same oil stained khaki jumpsuit and chomping on a rarely lit Cuban cigar, he spent his weekends working on his nuclear arsenal. He would put us to work stenciling the red stars and the CCCP logo on the missiles. There was a fridge out there stocked with Yoo-hoo and Grape Nehi for us, but he sternly reminded us that the homemade vodka on the top shelf was only for him to drink. And to run the lawn mower with. In a box under the workbench there were several dozen bundles of unused rope. Once, when I asked about this, he just chuckled and said that was the rope he buys with which he will one day hang us. He joked like that a lot.

One day, he got a new centrifuge for enriching uranium, which he purchased with S&H Green Stamps. He was excited as a kid on a secular Christmas morning as he carefully assembled it while insisting that it was just as good as the Craftsman model at Sears. Rather than showing us how it worked, he bored us with a detailed explanation of the economic model for Green Stamps. How you got them for free based on how much untaxable food and household goods you bought at the grocery store. And when you had collected enough you could go to the redemption center, which was like a small department store, to buy appliances, sporting goods, and yard furniture. He marveled in its sheer brilliance and said this would someday trigger the downfall of capitalism, as the proletariat would abandon the market-based economy that we were all forced fed. Charlie and I didn't press the validity of this point; we just nodded in agreement hoping he'd finish so we could see that cool new centrifuge ramp up to full RPM.

Really the only ugly incident I remember happened one Labor Day. Kroozie set up a podium (which I'm pretty sure he purchased with Green Stamps) down at the Safeway entrance, where he spoke loudly and angrily in Russian while pounding on the podium with his shoe. A few people stopped to watch but most hurried by, clearly disturbed by the embarrassing spectacle. Mothers sheltered their children, an old man threatened to call his Congressman, and a Filipino man interrupted him to ask him if he knew where the nearest Esso station was. After an hour or so he packed up and left. None of the neighbors ever brought it up, and as far as I know nothing like that ever happened again.

I was in 8th grade when he died. An ambulance showed up at 7 AM and a bunch of the neighbors gathered on the sidewalk in front of his house. When the EMTs rolled Kroozie by us on the stretcher he was hooked up to tubes and IVs and pretty much looked like sickle-and-hammered shit. Seeing Charlie and me, he smiled feebly and waved. Then reached up and pulled his oxygen mask away and said, "You boys to be good men. Spacibo, comrades." In unison, we gave him a somber "Poka, Kroozie," and that was it. They loaded him into the ambulance and we never saw or thought much about him again.

Many years later I phoned with my mother who still lives in the same old house off Fairhaven that I grew up in. When I asked her about the neighborhood, she said the people who lived in Kroozie's old house had recently sold and moved away. She added that the new owner was a tall bearded man who said he was from Saudi Arabia.

DAGNABBIT

Steve Bedle

A single white hair rises above the rest of my brow,
an ominous spire towering over a village.
Soon they will all be that way;
a crunchy grey forest fire crinkling atop glasses
as I peer down at the bottom of a grocery receipt,
confused, while the cashier impatiently points
at my double coupon savings for the third time,
my teeth bared between slack jaw and scrunched nose,
hair mussed at the cowlick, the sleeves of the loose-fitting
maroon v-neck sweater pushed up to my forearms
from fishing for Werthers at the bottom of my khaki pockets.
It is a future I'm not ready to admit so I yank, not pluck—
in keeping with my manscape ban—and banish
the stray hair to the bathroom sink. The mirror fogs
and unfogs. I notice the tiny blond cilia sprouting
from my ear, whispering to me that my Buick
is already rolling downhill.

Blue Spaces

Amanda Byzak

He never looked at me.
As he nursed, his eyes went to other places.
"Oh, he's fine," they said.

Still, he never looked at me.

From the corner of my eye,
I watched closely, others—
happy faces, looking at each other.
"He is not fine," I said.

Yet, the pediatrician looked and looked again.
Shrugged.
"He's fine," he said.

Everyone reassured me.
But inside I was a bit crazy.

Months went by.

Then, the eye doctor looked and looked again.
"He's blind," he said.

I laughed. My husband cried.
"See, he's not fine," we said.

Everyone reassured me.
But inside I was a bit crazy.

Months went by.

Then, he looked at me! For a flicker of a second. I swear it!
        Or am I crazy?

The eye doctor looked and looked again.
"He is not blind!" he said.

Years went by.

And after blood tests,
glasses, eye surgery,
IEPs, vision therapies,
orientation and mobility,
large print, magnifiers,
pre-canes, Braille,
and a blue parking placard
we are fine.

Yet, I am still a bit crazy.

THE JOURNEY HOME

Carolyn Budd

Sergio wiped his forehead
and spat on the hardened ground.
There was no water for him
to drink and his throat was sore.

His brother had warned him not
to leave his family behind.
"You will be hungry for home
and the dollar is poison."

He unwrapped stale tortillas
from his bandana. He could
still smell Rosa's jasmine soap,
her hand soothing his forehead.

The sickness rose from the field.
It burned his eyes, split his tongue.
He heard Rosa's voice—the warmth
of her breath overcame him.

Sergio sat in the dirt.
He bit his cheek and the blood
ran down his throat. His lips brimmed
blue-red in the cold white sun.

He saw Rosa in the sky,
circling high above him.
"Come home, my sweet love," she sighed.
"Oh, luminous earth, open wide."

BILLY JOE

Gary Winters

BILLY JOE KEPT PUTTING HIS HEAD on the bar. But what the heck, it was an after-hours joint, sort of like a private club. So it weren't no surprise to see folks looking like they'd been drinking for twelve hours straight. Still talking loud though. Kind of loose is how I'd describe it.

Billy Joe said he'd been kicked out of his room so I let him come to my place. Next day I helped him collect his suitcases. He ended up staying on because he never had any money. Had plenty of nice clothes though. We were the same size. He slept on my couch. I wore his clothes. He had a way with women, a real charmer. Good looking, hazel-green eyes, wavy blonde hair. A more amiable guy you'd never meet.

A couple months later I asked Billy Joe why he never dated a woman didn't have an old man. He touched his nose. "That's my escape hatch. If it gets too serious she can't complain when I decide it's time to cut out. She's already taken, see?"

•

One night we were drinking tequila shooters at a Mex bar. Billy Joe spots this señorita across the room and saunters over. Casual but direct. He brings her back to the table and jumps right in with both Tony Lama cowboy boots. I can't say I blamed him. The gal was slim but wiry, like she could hold her own in a cat fight. She was more than all right. Dark gold eyes, long black hair. And a skirt so skimpy that all you saw was brown legs, legs, legs.

Billy Joe's eyeing the tattoo on her shoulder. "Who's Jaime? You still with him?"

"Oh, yes. We're still together."

Billy Joe licked his lips. This was too good to be true. They left after drinking a pitcher of Margaritas.

Billy Joe shows up next day looking dazed. Or maybe still drunk. I had to say it. "You meet up with Jaime?"

"Yeah," is all he said.

I find out later she had more tattoos she showed him that night. Four tattoos total, scattered around in places on her tight little body. The names of her children. That's how Billy Joe ended up with a wife and four kids.

¡AY, CARAMBA!

Jill G. Hall

I never thought much about cowboys
until he pushed into the *cantina*,
tight fringed chaps the color of Fall buckwheat.

Boots clomping and spurs jangling,
unshaven face like a prickly pear cactus.
But his smile as big and bright as a meadow.

I fling back my *mantilla*-covered head.
Breast mounds exposed above red corset
like two roses in full bloom.

One hand on my waist,
the other snaps a fan.
Heel on rail-back *silla*
I show him rough lace on thigh.

How could he strut right past me,
up to the bar and order himself a cold one?

THE CENTER OF THE UNIVERSE

Linda Hutchison

The universe does not revolve
around you says my friend,
puzzling me for days.

Summer has shut itself down
like a cold slab of marble and
there is no sun for either of us.

We crawl along like snails
hoping our shells will scrape rock,
ignite us like little rockets.

Secretly I scheme to rise up on
this slimy trail, ride it like a silver tail
into a new galaxy, named after me.

These extravagant claims are
temporary. My attempts at getting
mountains to push me up into the sky

have failed so far. I know I could be
plucked off this slippery path
at any time.

Messages in the Sand

Cate Shepherd

I'm standing outside my office with Sandra the nurse, when a waist high blur of color zooms past. He roars like a wild beast, and his red cape sails behind him as he dashes into the playroom.

"It's one of those cloth napkins left over from the holiday banquet," Sandra confesses with a sheepish smile. "I pinned it to his t-shirt collar."

Luke was the most popular five-year-old at St. Jerome's, a receiving home and treatment center for abused children in San Diego. I was the new Clinical Director, tasked with creating treatment programs for children and a new training program for therapists.

Wiry, freckle-faced, and funny, Luke tore through the halls every day with sound effects loud enough for a much bigger boy. His superhuman energy exhausted his caregivers, and we all grew more attached to him because he was such a handful.

Luke loved Batman and talked about him nonstop. In his little cape, he became Batman. Sometimes his flights of fantasy made his caregivers nervous. They were familiar with PTSD, but none of them had met a child with delusions and hallucinations before.

One afternoon in the playroom, Luke became an evil king who terrorized the younger children. "You will do as I say or you will die! Bow before me!" He swung his toy sword around fast, out of control, and hit his three-year-old brother, Nathan, in the face. Nathan screamed and cried.

"Luke! Put the sword down! Now!" Tony, the dorm supervisor shouted to snap Luke out of his trance.

"Bow before me, you little piece of shit!" Luke yelled at Tony and lunged at him with the sword. Tony grabbed it and wrapped his arms around Luke. He held the squirming little hellion in his lap till he calmed down. After a few minutes, Luke went limp and stared off into a black hole.

•

Dr. Peterson, the consulting psychiatrist, diagnosed Luke with childhood schizophrenia. This label made Luke exotic among his peers and intimidating to young therapists. After a few weeks of Luke's wild behavior, Dr. Peterson wanted to prescribe anti-psychotic medication.

Luke had been removed from his family at age four because of suspected abuse, but Children's Protective Services found no physical evidence. His medical records revealed little. And when Luke's fantasy life started to look more psychotic, Dr. Peterson's focus shifted from trauma to mental illness.

My old friend, Mark, Director of St. Jerome's, had become disgusted by the de-evolution of child psychiatry and called it the Disease of the Month Club. First it was ADD, then Bipolar Disorder. He objected when his psychiatry colleagues prescribed new, untested drugs to young children. "There is no way to predict how these medications might affect a child's brain," he said.

The psychiatry interns Mark supervised had not studied psychotherapy or psychodynamics in med school, and they paid little attention to a child's environment or relationships. "It's all about the meds now," Mark grumbled. "That's all they're trained to do."

At St. Jerome's, children's behavior was typically driven more by trauma and family dynamics than by mental illness, though the symptoms looked similar.

But if all you have is a DSM, everything looks like a mental disorder.

We were lucky to have a Medical Director like Mark who understood children in context, and did not rush to pathologize a traumatized child. And when he did prescribe medication, he prescribed therapy along with it to treat the underlying causes of symptoms.

Our clinical staff had been trained to do talk therapy, but that is not the language of young children.

I remodeled the abandoned restroom attached to my office and made it into a sandplay room. The sink and toilet were removed, leaving space for rows of toy shelves. I painted the inside of the bathtub aquamarine, and filled it with play sand. On three walls around the tub I painted a bright orange and red sunset.

The staff of St. Jerome's helped me fill the shelves with nature objects, symbols, and toys. This was a language children understood. Every week my new friends appeared at my office door bearing bundles like sacred offerings. Most of the objects were hand-me-down toys from their own children. Sandra the nurse went hiking on the weekends and brought in special rocks and pieces of wood.

•

One of Luke's rewards for good behavior was playing in the sand tub. He loved my collection of action figures and lost himself in the world of play. And though they adored him, the staff appreciated the break.

When Luke first visited the sand tub, he scooped dozens of toys off the shelves, loaded up his arms, and dumped them into the sand. He wasn't quite sure what to do after they were all in the tub.

I sat with him and sorted through the pile.

"Look! It's Batman!" I smiled at him.

"Yeah!" He snatched the action figure from my hand.

I rooted around some more. "Look! Ninja Turtles!"

He picked up one of the Ninja Turtles and examined him from all sides, while clutching Batman in his other fist.

We dug through the pile until Tony called him for dinner.

After Luke left, the sand looked like an archeological dig.

•

The following week in Case Conference, Dr. Peterson pushed for meds. He had fallen in love with the Childhood Schizophrenia Study at the university and its accompanying clinical trials. And, of course, the yummy lunches catered by pharmaceutical companies.

"I think it is important to get this boy started on medication as early as possible," Peterson said. "Children who are medicated younger have better outcomes. We can stop these patterns in the brain before they become intractable."

He made pronouncements as though they were facts, even though the medications had not been adequately tested. Our children served as lab rats.

A few years earlier, I had worked at the psych hospital where I learned that overwhelming experience can produce psychotic symptoms in children. I remembered Maria, a straight-A student and track star, who became floridly psychotic, almost catatonic, after her long struggle to keep incest secrets. Her healthy, high-functioning nervous system reached a melting point and broke down. Medication didn't help until she spilled the secrets that had derailed her.

Dr. Peterson saw Luke twice for fifteen minutes before prescribing an anti-psychctic.

Sandra the nurse tried to stall him. "He's awfully young to take such a strong drug," she said. "And he's so tiny. There must be some other way we can help him."

I chimed in. "I think we should do a more thorough assessment before we medicate a five-year-old with anti-psychotics. Luke's behavior could be disorganized for a lot of reasons. He's a very imaginative little boy. And we don't know what kind of trauma he's been through."

Dr. Peterson frowned. He looked down and scribbled on his prescription pad. Everyone knew that Mark backed me up when I disagreed with the consulting psychiatrists. Dr. Peterson was nice enough, but he was sort of a one-trick-pony when it came to treating trauma. "Well, we can wait till next week if you want to observe him a little longer," he said. "Who's next?" He went down the list of children, assuming that each one needed at least one prescription.

•

The next time Luke came to play, he picked out a few superheroes, some soldiers and tanks, and made war. I couldn't make much sense of his noisy battle, but it seemed cathartic. He lost himself in play. Bombs exploded, warriors shouted, Batman roared.

Sand swished through the air and smacked against the painted walls. Some of it flew out of the tub. Luke stirred it around on the floor with his busy little body.

•

The following week when Luke came to play, he grabbed a red and blue rocket ship, about ten inches long, in his tiny right hand. In his left hand, he held a small Batman action figure.

With the fury of a madman, Luke thrust the rocket into Batman's little bottom again and again. He channeled a deep, gruff voice that I had never heard before

"Fuck you, bitch! Shut up, bitch! I'll give you something to cry about!" He looked possessed.

Chills shuddered through my body.

Luke smacked Batman around with the rocket.

I knelt beside him on the sandy floor and laid my palm between his shoulder blades. "Hey, Luke, what's happening?" I spoke in a soft voice.

Luke was in a trance. He stopped shouting, but continued to poke Batman and whispered, "Stupid bitch. Piece of shit."

Sorrow swelled in my throat.

•

My art therapist friend, Terri, came to St. Jerome's to teach the new psychotherapy interns how to do Sandplay Therapy. She brought three shoeboxes full of magical sandplay miniatures from her collection: witches, unicorns, Hindu gods, dragons, Mary and Jesus, angels and devils. She even gave me her favorite piece: The Sandplay Wizard. He stood about four inches tall and wore a purple robe with white fur trim. In his outstretched hands he held a magic wand and a crystal ball. His bewitching grin looked so real, I expected him to say something.

Terri taught us about right brain interventions and how they can bypass the defenses to directly access unconscious material. She told us stories about children who had worked through traumatic experiences by playing them out in the sand tray week after week.

Terri said children are pre-programmed to heal themselves. All we have to do is create and hold a safe play space for them. And keep our own agendas out of the way.

"Sandplay is like wakeful dreaming," she said, "with its archetypal symbols and unconscious meanings. The child's internal world is represented in the sand."

Terri asked me to present Luke's case as an example for the interns. I told them about our play, and about the controversy over his diagnosis.

"How old was he when they found him?" Terri asked.

"Four," I said. "CPS suspected sexual abuse by the father, but they didn't find any physical evidence. The mother had died, and Luke and his two-year-old brother were neglected for several months before a report came in."

Terri scrunched up her forehead and propped her fingers over her mouth.

"They said he went completely nuts when they tried to do a rectal exam."

Terri's frown deepened. "He may not have words for what happened to him if he was traumatized before he had the language to make sense of it. But he has body memories."

I nodded. "I'm not sure how best to help him with his play," I said. "He gets pretty psychotic at times. I don't want to re-traumatize him."

"Stay connected with him while he plays," Terri said. "Be very present and follow his lead. You'll know what to do."

"Just trust the Force, eh?"

"Yeah, that's it. The Force." Terri smiled. The interns laughed.

•

Terri would never accept payment for her workshops, so I rewarded her that evening with homemade pizza and Kendall Jackson Cabernet. We sat on the deck behind my beach cottage and watched the surfers while my Shih Tzu puppy bounced around in the grass.

We chatted and laughed while the sun set. Surfers still straddled their boards in wet suits when it became too cold for us to sit outside.

As she was packing up to leave, Terri dug around in the back of her Jeep for some more sand play goodies she wanted to give me. Puffy, my redheaded outlaw kitty, jumped up into the Jeep and climbed into Terri's sand tray. It was about twice the size of Puffy's litter box and full of clean sand.

"Puffy! No!"

But it was too late. I gasped in horror.

Terri just laughed and scooped out the sand.

•

The next morning, I cleared a spot for Terri's magical sandplay wizard on the top shelf. I could use all the help I could get.

Luke came to see me twice a week. He played out the same scene over and over. He assaulted Batman with the rocket, smacked him around and berated him.

One afternoon while I watched Luke's play, I scanned the shelves for an ally. Spiderman, Catwoman, Hulk, Hercules . . . Luke Skywalker! Perfect.

Nervous about how Luke might react to my intrusion, I approached with care.

"Uh oh, Rocket . . . you're in trouble now." I held Luke Skywalker up and waited for Luke's reaction.

He whipped his head around and looked startled. His eyes grew wide and his breathing sped up.

Uh oh.

He stared at the toy in my hand with the tunnel vision of fight-flight.

"Luke Skywalker is coming to save Batman. Vvvh! Vvvh!" I made light saber sounds.

Luke snapped out of his trance and looked at me. He grinned and sat up straighter.

"Take that, Rocket! Vvvh! Vvvh!" I smacked the rocket with Luke Skywalker's light saber.

Luke chuckled, and tightened his grip on the rocket.

"Come with me, Batman! The shuttle is waiting!" I gently pulled Batman out of Luke's sweaty little hand. He didn't resist.

"Here we go! I grabbed a space ship off the shelf and zoomed them away to safety. "Vroom!"

Sand crunched under Luke's boot as he pivoted to watch the ship. His intelligent blue eyes tracked Batman. He didn't say a word, but dropped the rocket into the tub.

The rocket lay upside down, engulfed by sand, surrounded by Luke's allies.

•

The next time Luke came to play, he rescued Batman with Catwoman. In the weeks that followed, he rescued him with Spiderman, Hulk, and Hercules. Sometimes they all piled on.

After Luke's allies rescued Batman a few times, Batman fought Rocket on his own. And, after Batman kicked Rocket's ass for a few weeks, Luke's rage faded. His play became calmer and more contained. He was able to keep all of the sand inside the tub.

•

When Dr. Peterson saw Luke for his quarterly follow-up he noted the absence of delusions and hallucinations, and stopped talking about schizophrenia. But he wanted to prescribe the new drug for ADHD.

One afternoon while Luke played, he smacked Rocket hard against the side of the tub and broke him in two. He gasped and looked up at my face with wide eyes, clutching Rocket's tail in his hand.

"Ah ha! Take that, Rocket!" I shouted and clapped my hands.

Luke chuckled his deep, funny chuckle, and looked down at the broken toy.

"Now what do we do?" I asked.

"Leth bury him!" He sprayed through his missing tooth. His eyes sparkled above a lopsided grin.

I grabbed a plastic shovel and scooped out the sand. Luke dug with his hands. We dug a deep hole, big enough for lots of rockets.

I placed the broken rocket pieces in Luke's palms. He looked at them for a moment, then dropped them into the bottom of the pit and shoved sand on top of them and patted it flat.

The smooth sand looked so peaceful.

•

Mark taught us that trauma was determined by the response of the environment. Kids could survive horrible injuries, losses, and despair if they didn't feel alone. Empathy and validation helped them metabolize their experiences.

But children who were left alone with overwhelming pain and fear became far more disrupted. Without connection and support, traumatic memories remained raw, unprocessed, and easily triggered.

We never learned what happened to Luke before we met him, but he was no longer alone in his nightmare.

A few weeks later, Luke brought his little brother to play. Nathan's long, blonde curls formed a cherubic afro, and he wore fat, padded pull ups instead of pants.

I greeted them at the door. "Hey, guys. Wanna check out my new toys?"

"Yeah!" Luke yelled.

"Yeah!" Nathan mimicked.

Luke grabbed Nathan's hand and led him into the sandplay room. "Look!" He held up the Batman action figure. "Batman ith the motht powerful! Grr!"

Nathan plopped his padded bum down on the sandy floor and watched his big brother. Luke introduced each of the superheroes and explained their powers. For a moment, he seemed so grown up.

Nathan stood, scooped an armful of toys off a shelf, and dumped them into the tub.

"No!" Luke yelled. "Nathan!" Luke propped his fists on his hips and shook his head. He looked up at me with an exasperated expression. "I'll thow him how to do it."

Luke sorted through the pile in the tub and put some of the toys back on the shelf.

"Here, Nathan, you can be in charge of the soldiers." Luke picked soldiers out of the pile and showed them to his brother. Nathan picked up a soldier and studied it.

Luke shoved the pile to the foot of the tub and lined up soldiers and tanks for a proper war.

It was a hot summer afternoon, and I stood near the doorway of the playroom to catch the breeze that blew in through the open windows.

Luke cackled as he smacked soldiers and tanks together. Sand flew and swished against the sides of the tub.

Nathan picked up fistfuls of sand and watched it cascade through his chubby fingers. He giggled at Luke's noisy play.

These kids had a gift for creating moments of joy while going through hell.

After a few minutes of rowdy play, Luke grew bored. "Hey, Nathan, leth go play thordfight!"

He looked at me. I nodded, and he scampered out the door with baby brother trailing behind.

I looked around the playroom and remembered the afternoons I had spent with Luke. The light seemed brighter than before. It was that late afternoon low light that makes everything glow. I picked the toys out of the tub and returned them to their shelves. The warm sun beamed in and animated tiny metallic specks in the sand as I raked it smooth.

As I rose to leave, a flash of light startled me. Terri's grinning wizard sat on the top shelf among Luke's action figures. His crystal ball refracted a sunbeam.

I grinned back at him and planted him in the glowing sand where he belonged.

Paris Morning

Claire Accomando

Six thirty, and my cousin slips soundlessly out of the
apartment. I hear her downsteps on the stairs. The wind
parts the curtains. Between the brick-red geraniums of the
fourth floor window, I see Mariette on the street below,
elegant, high-heeled, younger than her years.

Seven o'clock, the scent of oven-warm bread precedes
her as she sneaks back in, hugging a baguette and a bag full
of golden croissants. My sisters and I dress quickly, drawn
to the table where red and blue bowls of frothy coffee await us.
We are the American cousins, visiting after thirty years.

We sip, cradling our bowls with both hands. We apologize for
being so many sisters. There are four of us. Our first trip together
since we were kids. Mariette is putting us up. She passes the apricot
jam. *It's good to have you,* she says. *Now that I'm alone, this place
is too silent. I miss the morning noises. I miss the voices.*

We pull apart the flaky flesh of the croissants and release the buttery
smell that nourishes the breeze. In the street, bumpers bang as drivers
pivot their parked cars inch by inch out of their tight spaces. Over
refills, we plan our day. We drink slowly and pick crumbs off the
cross-stitched table cloth to savor the moment for future decades.

PUBLIC SCHOOL

Elizabeth Trude

We were the tiniest teachers in school.
Mad little fingers and hurried hands scribbling notes
Making fun of the principal.

Pointless meetings headed by morons.
I drew naked pictures of the guest speaker.

One staff meeting morning,
You smelled like bed
And I crinkled my nose and kept my distance.

You were quiet, but I liked the poems you wrote.
I was snarky and bold and made you laugh.

Mr. Johnson, I thank you . . .
Your bald head, beautiful eyes and bitter words
Made public school bearable.

MEMORIAL DAY

William Cass

M ITSURU TOLD HIS WIFE THAT HE'D do the shopping for dinner. That was partly due to his wanting to share the chores, but mostly because of the way he'd found her the night before.

Esther hung the strap of her purse over her walker handle and began the slow, one block journey to the grocery store. The sun had dipped just below the treetops, the sky inky blue; it had been Bert's favorite part of the day.

Todd checked on his mother one last time before riding his bike to his job bagging groceries. She'd fallen asleep again in her recliner, her chin on her chest. He took the burning cigarette from between her fingers and stubbed it out. He left the beer can in her hand, but used the remote to turn off the television before he left.

Mitsuru parked along the street in front of the store. He got a cart inside and consulted the list she'd given him: all traditional bar-b-que items—hot dogs, hamburgers, potato salad, corn on the cob, watermelon.

The night before, he'd found that she wasn't in bed next to him at about 3:00 AM. He followed the light to the end of the hall where she sat at the kitchen table. A bottle of white wine was on the table, and she held a juice glass full of it on her knee.

Softly, he said, "Hey."

She turned, startled, and put a hand that clenched a tissue to her chest. Her eyes were wide, red-rimmed with tears.

"It's only been a few weeks," he said. "Nothing to worry about yet. He's probably fine."

Mitsuru was referring to their son who'd enlisted in the Marines with a buddy on a dare the day after they'd graduated from high school the year before. He'd been deployed in Helmand province in Afghanistan for the past five months. Except for the last month, he'd always found a way to call or send an email each week to let them know he was safe.

Esther made her way through the parking lot and in through the back entrance of the grocery store. She hung a black plastic basket on the opposite handle from her purse on the walker. Her path through the store was premeditated and methodical; she got lentil soup, instant coffee, nighttime pain reliever, and then fixings for strawberry shortcake.

She was pleased to find the line short at the express lane and the nice boy bagging at the end of it.

Todd smiled and gave a little wave to Esther as she entered the line. Then he craned his neck again to see if the girl from his math class had rounded the end of the frozen food aisle.

She'd come in with her ditzy friend. They both wore bikini tops, cut-off jean shorts, and flip-flops. She was tall and long-legged, and her friend was squat. She'd asked him for help with a problem in class the week before and had smiled and thanked him when he'd finished doing that.

Her eyes were kind. He'd watched the girls giggle over some singing greeting cards before heading toward the frozen foods. If they'd noticed him, they gave no indication of it.

Mitsuru peeled back the husks on the corn a bit, and then satisfied, twisted them into a plastic bag and dropped them in the cart. They were his last items. He remembered suddenly his grandmother telling him as a boy how the other young girls and herself had tended a garden that included corn in their Japanese internment camp in central California during World War II. That was where his wife's mother and his own had first met as children and had become lifelong friends.

The truth was that, with their families' histories, they were both reluctant about their son joining the military. Mitsuru thought that if his wife were pressed for truthfulness, she would say that she was opposed to it; in fact, full of regret and bitterness. Although he expressed nothing but pride publically about his son's decision, if he were pressed himself, he didn't know for sure how he would respond.

Esther knew the man checking her groceries well. He passed her items down to Todd after scanning them, and then told Esther the total. She rummaged through her purse until she came upon her money clip. But, it clenched only a ten dollar bill and two ones. She gave those to the checker and mumbled, "Sorry."

He held the bills between his fingers and smiled. "What do you want to start taking away today, Mrs. Meyers?"

"Well," she said. "I can do without the whipped cream."

He took the can, set it next to the cash register, and punched some keys. "All right. What next?"

"Well, I guess the strawberries will be fine by themselves." She handed him the spongy cake cups in their cellophane.

He punched a few more keys, looked at her sheepishly and said, "Almost there."

Esther was a short woman; her head didn't come much higher than his key pad. She had to reach to get to the strawberries and hand them to him. He made the calculations, smiled at her, and said, "Okay, you're fine now."

A few coins slid down the mechanism that Esther collected and dropped in her purse.

Todd had her items ready in the plastic sack she favored.

"Do you need help out today, Mrs. Meyers?"

"No, dear," she said. "I'll be fine."

Todd wrapped the sack over the free end of her walker handle. With only those few items, it was light. She patted his hand, smiled up at him, and said, "Thank you very much."

He watched her make her way toward the back door, and then turned his attention to the two girls who'd come up to the ice cream case. The one in his math class had taken out a Drumstick and was holding it wide-eyed at her friend. "I love these!" he heard her say.

Mitsuru had been two people behind Esther in the express line and had watched her exchange with the checker. When his turn came, he said, "Do you think it's too late to add those things for that older woman to my bill?" He nodded at the strawberry shortcake items sitting next to the cash register. "Could you ring them quickly and catch her?"

The checker traded glances with Todd, then shrugged and said, "Well, she doesn't move very fast, and she only lives up the block. Runs a dance studio that's become a bed-and-breakfast. Or at least, that's what it used to be. Todd, can you see if you can catch up to Mrs. Meyers if I run these things?"

"Sure," the boy said. From the corner of his eye, he saw the two girls leave the store to the street without buying anything.

The checker scanned the items, and then Todd ran quickly out the back door with them.

He caught up to Esther as she was entering her front walk.

"Mrs. Meyers," he said when he'd come up beside her, a little breathless. "A man bought you these. A man in line behind you."

Todd held up the clear plastic carton of strawberries in one hand and the can of whipped cream and cake shells in the other. "Here," he said more slowly and put them in the bag on her walker.

Esther's frown of bewilderment and surprise softened into a smile. Her shoulders dropped, and she said, "Well, isn't that something?"

"Yes," Todd said. "It is."

"How can I thank him?"

"I'm afraid he's gone by now, Mrs. Meyers. I didn't recognize him."

"Well, isn't that something? Isn't that something grand?"

"Yeah, I guess it is."

"It is, young man. And you'd better remember it. It's something special, and it's something grand. You don't see something like that very often. It's made my day, I can tell you that."

Todd nodded. He followed her to the front door, and held it open for her. He figured that she was about thirty years older than his mother. He hoped to attend community college once he was done with high school, and then the local university afterward so he could still take care of her. He didn't know what would happen after that.

Mitsuru set places on the picnic table on the back porch for dinner while he barbecued and his wife sent their son another email. They didn't talk much over dinner. Afterwards, his wife went to take a bath, and he cleaned up slowly. He was aware of the falling light of evening, a time when he and his son often used to play catch in earlier years. He thought that Esther was probably about the same age as his mother would have been if she'd still been alive.

Esther ate her soup from the pot at her dining room table. As she did, she looked at some of the framed photos on the wall: she and Bert when they were in the same summer stock musical production after college in Connecticut; Bert, still a young man, sitting at the piano in one of the places he'd found work after they'd moved to San Diego; a few of her with her hair done-up long ago in dance ensembles on both coasts; a couple of him in later years in his garden outside; one of the two of them eating lobster with friends down in Puerto Nuevo a long time ago.

She'd left his gardening tools in the shed after he'd died. That back area was now mostly full of junk: discarded items from the dance studio, tools, broken furniture, a rusted hammock from better days. She hadn't had a dance student in over twenty years, and only a few old time customers came to stay at the bed-and-breakfast anymore, perhaps a handful a year.

Todd stayed on a little after closing to stock shelves for another worker who'd gotten the night off for the holiday. The deli guy passed on some of the remaining fried chicken and potato wedges to him before he left that would otherwise be thrown away. Todd used a little of the tip money he'd been saving to buy a patriotic bouquet for his mom, as well as a Drumstick.

When he got home, Todd found her sleeping as he'd left her, but there were two new empty beer cans next to the recliner, and the television was on again. He tried to roust her for some dinner, but she waved him away and fell back asleep. He turned off the television again and put the flowers in a vase, arranging the tiny American flag it held so that it stood straight up in the middle. Then he ate the chicken and potatoes from their paper sack on the front step while he thought about how to get the Drumstick to the girl at school the next day.

They all heard the fireworks begin at the same time: a special show across the bay at Petco Park after the baseball game. Esther watched from her bedroom window. Mitsuru returned to the back porch; his wife had already gone off to bed. Todd stayed where he was on the front step.

It was a big show for the holiday and went on for some time. Pops in the distance preceded the draping sprays of colored lights high in the sky. When the fireworks ended, a vague cloud rose and dissipated over the bay, like the thought of the exchange at the grocery check-out already had for the three of them. However, it would be something they would all think about from time to time, at odd moments, more often than they might have imagined. Each of them had different reasons for that, but the most important ones were the same.

BERKELEY SOUP KITCHEN

Joan Gerstein

In the garish light of a soup kitchen they meet.
Hands shake while he holds the plate. His eyes
boldly fixing her in their sight while she ladles
Sunday's meal, giving him extra. He sits on a tan
Naughahyde chair, crusty with crumbs, laced
with cuts and burns, his eyes devouring her.

He offers to help clean up to be closer to her,
his new friend, his fantasy girlfriend. She smiles
broadly at him, safe in a public place. She likes him,
he can tell. Hands touch as pans pass from water
to towel. They talk, they laugh, until evening
returns her to a house, him to the streets.

Every day they meet over meals but do not break
bread together. The Vietnam War, madness,
substance abuse create a chasm too great to climb.

Under concrete bridges he dreams. Her silk body
touches his. He buries his hopes in auburn
tresses where Paradise is at his fingertips.
Awake he writes her poems on scraps of paper,
sides of grocery bags. Finally their daily meetings
bolster him bold enough to share a few poems. Her
eyes first sparkle in delight, then grow large in fright.

The next week, she's not at the soup kitchen. He knows
it is because of him, his sickness, poverty, neediness.
She will not return while he is there. It's time to hoist
his hardships and get on down the road.

THE TALE OF CYRIL, THE FRIENDLY RUSSIAN SKINHEAD

David Schmidt

I CAN STILL SEE THE WHOLE scene as if it were yesterday: twenty or thirty shaven heads were glistening under the single street lamp. The sea of navy blue bomber jackets and black boots stood out in sharp contrast against the freshly fallen snow. I stared at the crowd through the peephole on the door of the Baptist church; the curved glass distorted their features, making them look like grotesque creatures from a Hieronymus Bosch painting.

We knew this was coming—we had been worried about the skinheads for a while.

When Grant and I left sunny California in 2003 to do volunteer work in Russia, Fascism was not on our list of concerns. We rented an apartment in the southern Russian town of Engels and split our time between Engels and the neighboring city of Saratov. Our days were spent teaching English, volunteering at children's camps, hosting musical events, and organizing youth groups with a local Baptist church. We spent at least half of our time trying to locate our apartment complex at the end of each day, nestled as it was in a sea of identical buildings.

All said and done, it was a fairly leisurely life at first. We had even found a fast food joint that made greasy slider-style burgers, topped with freeze-dried onions and nearly edible curry sauce.

One of the first rumblings of danger came when we returned to Engels' drab cityscape from a church summer camp. The Baptists' bus was pulling up to the church, circumnavigating the constellations of potholes in the road, when we saw a two-word graffito written on the church door—"bei zhidov"—employing a Russified version of the slur "Yid." It translated as "let's stomp some kikes." (What anti-Semitism had to do with a Baptist church, I couldn't figure out.) Most of the church kids brushed it off as senseless vandalism. Valera, the youth group leader, sneered at the tagging and dismissed it with a real zinger of a comeback. "Oh yeah? Bei zhidov, huh? Well bei skinhead-ov!" He leaned back with a self-satisfied look on his face.

The dark clouds of hostility continued to gather that autumn, when Grant and I went to Berlin to renew our Russian visas. We returned to Moscow's Sheremetevo Airport, fat and happy from German bratwurst and beer, and turned on our Russian cell phone. I checked our text messages. One text from a morbidly obese Mormon man who was in love with us. Another from one of our English students. And a message from the young Baptists who co-led our youth group:

Grant and David: be careful. 25 skinheads came to the church last night. They are looking for you.

I texted Oksana back:

Ha ha. I'm sorry Oksana, I almost thought for a second you'd said that twenty-five skinheads were looking for us.

We met up with Oksana, Natasha, and several others, and all of them confirmed the story: a crowd of radical nationalists had shown up for church youth group on Tuesday, looking for the "foreigners" who worked there. Just my luck, I thought. I don't run into Nazis until after I've left Germany. Welcome to the Europe of the twenty-first century.

Grant and I kept a low profile that week. We did drop by our friends' local rock café, since they had invited us to their heavy metal concert on Halloween night. We slunk in through the back door and sat at a table in the shadows, watching intently as a ponytailed man at our table sifted through a brick of Kazakh weed. Suddenly, we heard a familiar voice behind us. "Oh ho ho, David! Grant! Yes-shit-fuck-U.S.A.!" Trouba, the club's owner, only knew four words in English; he did us the courtesy of reciting them in no particular order every time he saw us.

"I'm so glad you boys could come down," he slurred in Russian. Google-eyed and constantly drunk, Trouba looked like a goofier version of the actor Marty Feldman. "Wait here a second," he said as he headed toward the stage.

We went back to discussing the intricacies of Russian "homegrown" with our table companion, when the music suddenly stopped and Trouba's voice came screeching through the speakers. "I hope you're all enjoying the concert. As you all know, today is Halloween, and Halloween is an American holiday. And it just so happens that we have two real, live Americans in our midst tonight. Their names are Grant and David and they're sitting at that table right over there. Stand up, lads! Take a bow! Shit-yes-U.S.A.-fuck!"

As the spotlight zoomed in on Grant and me, I noticed someone eyeing us from a nearby table. He was leaning back with his linebacker-sized arms crossed over his chest, wearing black steel-toed boots, a bomber jacket, and a scary-as-hell Halloween mask. "Who's our friend over here with the body-by-Thor?" I asked an acquaintance.

"Oh, Vasya? He's just the leader of the local skinheads." I glanced back over. Vasya was still staring at me through the empty holes in his rubber monster head, immobile. He didn't seem to even breathe the entire night. Grant and I took Vasya's ominous presence as our cue to leave: we ducked out the back and took a shortcut home through the town cemetery, preferring to take our chances with the Halloween ghosts.

We knew we had to deal with the issue, though. The following Tuesday, we announced that youth group would be canceled. My Russian was finally fluent enough for me to facilitate the serious conversation of what to do about the skinhead problem. Grant and I met with our leadership team in the church kitchen one evening to devise a plan. Oksana and Misha favored shutting down the youth group for good, while Marina and Natasha suggested we try to dialogue with our would-be attackers.

The tea kettle had just started to whistle when we heard a tapping at the door.

Knock knock knock. "Open up."

I dropped my spoon into the sugar bowl. Natasha stood holding two dripping plates over the sink. Grant looked up from the Dictionary of Russian Profanity he had been studying. The book's cover silently screamed the Russian word for "Shit!"

Knock knock knock. "We know you've got foreigners in there. Open the door."

The kettle kept screeching.

We all crowded around the church door. I edged my way to the front of the group and looked through the peephole. As I counted two dozen shaved heads, I muttered an Indiana Jones quote under my breath: Nazis. I hate these guys! The door rattled in my face as the knocks grew stronger.

I took a step back and steeled my face, putting on the best hard-ass Clint Eastwood expression I could muster. I grabbed the knob, swung open the heavy iron door, and glared resolutely into darkness. And nothing more.

Staring into the night's plutonian shore, I was ready to start believing in the witchcraft that Baptists commonly attributed to their enemies. The skinheads vanished into thin air! I thought. Then I looked downward.

A sea of tiny bald heads, miniature blue bomber jackets, polished boots, and tiny little fists of fury spread out before me. Most of the boys looked to be sixth graders. The whole scene was surreal, like something from a Tim Burton movie. At first, I thought my eyes were playing tricks on me; then I felt disappointed, like I'd been ripped off somehow. I wasted all that adrenaline on a bunch of mini-skinnies?

Still, twenty-five skinheads are twenty-five skinheads, pint-sized or otherwise, so we proceeded with caution. Marina (a lanky girl at least five times taller than most of these boys) asked if they went everywhere together, if they showered together and slept in one big cozy bed. Ah, irony—the natural enemy of racial hatred! The sixteen year old kingpin of the mini-skinnies eventually stepped forward; he introduced himself as Cyril, named after the charitable saint who invented the Russian alphabet. I guessed that he was the vandal who had misspelled the word "kike" in his graffito on the church door.

Cyril cracked his knuckles and stared up at me. His pimply face showed all the ferocity of a recently neutered Pomeranian. "So you're one of the foreigners, huh?" he asked me.

"Well, technically, my great-grandparents were from Russia, but then again they had a German last name, so I suppose it all depends on how you define 'foreigner' . . ."

"We don't like what's going on here in this church. We're patriots."

"What have you guys got against these Baptists, anyway?"

"Well, you know, um . . . Jesus was a Jew."

"I thought you Russians had forgotten that centuries ago! Look at how they paint him in your icons, man. You make him look totally white and Slavic."

"But we think our Fatherland should have a Slavic religion. You know, not a Jew religion."

"So you want to bring it back to the pre-Christian days of nature spirits and human sacrifice?"

"I want to burn my parents on a floating funeral pyre."

"That's the Vikings you're thinking of."

"Huh?"

"Besides, you should know that even Slavic paganism incorporated elements of Asian mythology centuries ago."

"Whuh?"

"The 'Tree of Life' concept—it comes from Siberia. May even be of Mongolian origin."

"Zuh?"

"Why don't you just come in for a cup of tea."

Cyril came inside to chat with us. Turns out, he was mostly harmless; once we had him alone, we found him to be just another nervous, confused kid. We invited him to come back to the church the following week. He did. He brought all his mini-skinnies with him. They played the ice-breaker game we organized, a relay race where teenagers passed an orange to each other with their chin. They had tea and cookies along with the other people in the youth group. They participated in the philosophical discussion we had planned.

The kids who had once inspired Grant and me to look over our shoulder as we walked around town eventually became a regular fixture at our youth group.

Beneath his tough exterior, Cyril ended up being a real mensch.

At 5 am

Anna DiMartino

the decision is
whether to make love
or coffee.
I set my knitting down
step lightly through
the living room
to the bedroom
and standing at the bed
let my robe fall to the floor.
The cotton sheets are cool
but you are warm.
You pull me close
wrap me
in your body.
You press your cheek
against mine.
I feel your breath
on my neck.
At 5am
the decision
is easy.

MORNING

Elizabeth Trude

Three minutes and five inches in
it finally dawns on him
that she is no longer there.

He likes a party
yet, the fresh wine on
her sour morning breath
no longer feels like fun.

Why are there stretch marks?
Where are the children?

He stays . . .
his eyes fixed on the door.
Her tender, crushing hurt
keeps him in place.

Last night it was thrilling,
romantic, tragic . . .
the careless notion of riding
this broken-down woman.

But now . . .

in this room that is oppressively brown,
it is only regrettable:
the loose threads in her nylon panties,
eyeliner bleeding into the creases beneath her eyes,
a missing molar, her greyish bra.

He strokes her stained fingers
and feels ashamed for them both.

The Porch

Olivia Tomkinson

He puts on his favorite blue sweater and grabs a beer
Walks down the hallway to the porch
I just need some time to think
he says to himself as he stares out into the water.
Sitting on the padded chair he raises his feet
and watches the lights in the sea as they flicker.

He notices the lights of boats in the distance flicker
and realizes that he wants another beer.
His legs contact the ground as he stands up on his feet
It's cool tonight, outside on the porch
and the rainfall collects in puddles of water
His eyes begin to cross as he thinks.

It's getting late, she must be home, he thinks,
this thought racing in his mind flickers
as he hears the sound of running water.
Going to the kitchen he picks up a beer.
Heading back out onto the porch,
He feels the hands of anxiety creep up as he sits and ties the shoes
       on his feet.

After a long day at work, she comes home and feels the weight of
 her tired feet
and decides to draw a bath, spending some time to think.
Walking to the door, she finds her husband on the porch
and watches as the wind causes the leaves on the trees to flicker.
She turns on her heel, walks to the fridge and decides on a beer,
and walks to the bathroom to soak in the warm water.

She takes a sponge and massages her body with the bubble-filled water
stretches her legs beyond the edge of the tub where she rests her feet
and takes a sip of beer.
She begins to wonder what he is thinking.
The candle on the edge of the bathtub flickers.
I should stop my mind from wandering and join him on the porch.

She gets out of the bath and walks to the door of the porch,
Listens to the rain as it falls and puddles in pools of water.
She stares, mesmerized, at the flames of the fire as they flicker.
She dresses in jeans and a warm sweater and puts shoes on her feet.
Wondering how to make an entrance, she thinks,
I will get us both a beer.

She steps onto the porch and they both smile as she hands him
 his beer
He takes her hand as they watch the water and the lights of the boats
 in the distance flicker
They abandon their thoughts and extend their legs to touch the
 other's foot.

RAPTURE: MAY 21, 2011

Ron Salisbury

Reverend Harold Camping predicted the "Rapture" would
occur on May 21, 2011 at 6 PM in each time zone.

On Rapture morning I take the dog
for his walk so he and the crows
can continue their ritual hatred.
The crows curse him from
the eucalyptus, swoop his head.
They know the exact length
of his leash, jeer when he jerks
up tight at the end. If he could
just fly, there would be trouble,
mouth full of feathers. If he could
he'd beg me to unclip his leash.

Reverend Camping spent his life
predicting our downfall. Judgment
would begin on the 21st
and those found lacking remain here
until the bloody end. The worthy
will rise up to Heaven. Some of us
remaining might panic, try to strike
a last minute deal. And others, resigned,
could experience Grace for the first time.

But this morning the world is quiet,
the park empty except for seven crows
by the lawn edge, huddled near
the eighth, dead in the grass;
some are in the low bushes, others
in a circle. The dog sits quietly
on the gravel path, watching,
then gets up and slowly
leads me out of the park.

NEWBORN CHICK

Lenise Andrade

I RUN UP THE SIDEWALK TO Kim's porch, take her in a full hug, and can't help myself—I run my hands all over her head. Her short pale red hair feels so soft, "like a newborn chick," she had said, but it reminds me more of a soft puppy, freshly washed.

"Look at you! I love it!" I tell her, glad that I fought through Valentine's Day traffic on the 405 to see her and her new home with Don. A corny heart-themed housewarming was just hours away, and just what everyone needed.

"Look at that parking!" she squeals, looking over my shoulder. "Seriously, how do you always get such good parking?"

"Parking? Really? After all you've been through, you want to talk parking?"

"Come on, it's LA. Everyone wants to talk parking!" She leads me inside the house with a playful grin.

We sit on her couch and drink tea, while she tells me the gory details. Her voice is brisk, yet calm as she reviews the past year, with a mix of candor and delivery worthy of a top-notch roast, but with slightly more graphic subject matter. The chemo, the fatigue, the night sweats, the cording . . .

"So, there were cords that come out of your pits?" I'm trying not to laugh, but watching her smirk as she shares makes it hard.

"Not really. Tissue in your underarms gets stiff and doesn't want to stretch anymore. You can't see it but it hurts like a bitch! It's like having tight wings, but you can't fly, so what's the point? Again, things they don't tell you at the beginning. WebMD became my best friend during those first few months."

And luckily her treatment was all at Cedars Sinai, and she has an awesome surgeon, who is making her an impressive pair of nipples.

"One male nurse there said they were the best he'd ever seen. Which was great, because I figured the female nurses were just being nice. And they're tattooing areolas on me! Did you know it was done as a tattoo? It's pretty funny, because it will actually be my first tattoo." She grins as she blows on her already cooled tea and tells me more.

•

The visits to Cedars weren't always easy that year. ("A shitty year," Kim said, is how the doctor described it would be. "And she was right!") She could brace herself, via the web and emails from her doctor, about what to expect each visit: the treatment details, the side effects, even the estimated lengths of her visits and recommendations on parking. But the timing of her first day of radiation after the surgery was October 1st, and she was greeted at the lobby with waterfalls of pink décor. The nurses were all in pink, the front desk was trimmed with columns of pink balloons, a bouquet of pink roses towered at the nurse's station, and even the pen she used to sign in with was festooned with that ubiquitous pink ribbon swirl.

Kim was tired from chemo and still moving slowly from the surgery. Her mom had driven her, so she didn't want to cause a scene, but the last several months had been an ever-increasing rolling road, and this was to be the last detail. Several rounds of radiation, reconstructive surgery, and a few follow up visits and she could move on with her life. So she tried to be nice and bite her tongue as the perky (and annoyingly chesty) blonde nurse checking her in asked question after question, in a overtly practiced tone, about her doctor, her surgery date, her symptoms, her address, her email address. For Christ's sake, Kim thought, isn't this in the damn file? Isn't this what computers were for? But she answered each question calmly, with as little expression as possible, reserving her strength for the first treatment ahead. Best to save her reserve for that, not this Komen cheerleader with the pink ribbon earrings (with bright pink rhinestones, no less!) who she hoped would not be here next week.

"Okay, Ms. Anderson, looks like you're all set. Just head over to the waiting area, down this hall and to the left, and someone will be with you in just a few minutes." Kim just smiled, as "Thanks" could not find a way to her lips, when the bimbette had the nerve to follow up with, "And don't forget your Komen tote!" She lifted a large puff of pink cotton across the counter toward Kim, who refused to raise her arms. Forget the cording; she just really had no response to this.

"What's in the bag?" As annoyed as she was, she hoped her lip wasn't actually as curled up as it felt.

"Well, there's a t-shirt, some stickers, a lovely pen, and some self examination literature."

"I think I've already had enough examinations, thank you." Kim responded, tight lipped.

"Well, of course, but you could share it with your friends, maybe? It's October!" the nurse continued, unflinching in her bright demeanor despite Kim's glaring green eyes. "It's Breast Cancer Awareness Month!" Kim could hear the capitals with each word.

"I am sufficiently aware of breast cancer. You can keep the tote bag." Kim blinked once and walked down the hall.

•

She had been surprised by how fiercely her mom turned into *Terms of Endearment* with everyone after the surgery. Not that Nan was an uninvolved mom, but she was basically shy and usually let Kim handle her own details. Nevertheless, she had been at the hospital for all of the four days Kim was there, days that were a blur of morphine, weak soup, and bad TV. Kim couldn't imagine she was good company and the details of post-op weren't pretty. The first morning, she faintly heard her mom yelling at a nurse about her fluids. She wasn't sure what fluids she was talking about, but all the talk of fluids got her to thinking about peeing. She suddenly really needed to pee. And when her mom came back into the room, she told her just that.

"Well, you have a catheter honey, so go ahead and pee," Nan whispered back.

"Are you sure?"

"Well, I didn't see them put it in, but I'm pretty sure they did."

"Well, I don't want to pee in the bed, so make sure!"

"Well, I'm not going to look . . ." her mom said, looking out the open door for a familiar face. One that she hadn't just yelled at.

"Can I pee?!" Kim yelled out into the air, as loud as she could.

"What?!" yelled a nurse from the hallway.

"I need to pee! Can I pee?!" Kim yelled again.

"Yes, yes, you have a catheter, Ms. Anderson. Just pee," said a nurse, running in to stop the yelling. And pee she did, "like a silent racehorse" she told me, and it was the best she had felt in weeks.

Her mom had rented a room at a hotel nearby ("to give you some space, honey") for the two weeks after, coming early in the morning to help Kim in and out of bed (since Kim couldn't really use her arms or chest muscles to sit up), to make her small meals and tea throughout the day, and then to help her into bed at night. It was a routine that reminded Kim of when she was young and would have the flu, but now that she was taller than her mom and had been through all of this, she felt more like Baby Huey in the cartoons, too big to need this much help, but too weak to handle anything much more than this on her own.

One early evening, Kim fell asleep on the couch, so Nan went to a nearby liquor store to buy some wine, because, frankly, it had been a long week and she didn't have the meds Kim did. And though she didn't always like Kim's neighborhood, she suddenly appreciated the selection at Fairfax Liquor around the corner.

When she came back up the sidewalk, she saw a group of 30-somethings outside on the stairs smoking. Kim's apartment building was filled with others her age, who laughed too loud, stayed out too late for their age, and didn't seem to be making any plans to start a family. They stood on the steps, smoking their cigarettes, laughing and talking, and didn't even seem to notice that she was fumbling with Kim's key to the front door to the lobby. Finally, the key turned and so did she.

"You know, it's getting late and I would really appreciate it if you would finish your cigarettes and go inside for the night, because my daughter is upstairs recovering from cancer surgery and the last thing we need to hear—or smell—is all of you out here!" Kim heard her mother's outburst through the open living room window upstairs. Nan stormed inside the apartment silently, letting the wood door slam. Kim let out a restrained giggle and then sent a text to her friend who lived downstairs, whose party guests had just been yelled at: *Sorry about my mom. It's been a hard few weeks. But please have an extra glass for me!'*

•

The night before the surgery, Kim and Don spooned quietly in her bed and both held onto her breasts. They listened to the 'Rock Chick' station on Pandora she had created, so the night wouldn't be totally sappy, but both of them could not stop touching her boobs. Oddly, it didn't turn her on. Instead, it was reassuring to just feel them. Their weight in her hands, how Don's hands seemed to prefer the sides and hers the front, even how they sweated and had goosebumps at the same time.

When she had first been diagnosed, she had inappropriately lashed out at him, but he had held strong. In her defense, they had only been dating a few months at the time, and her track record hadn't been great where reliable men had been concerned. So, she was honest when she said if he was going to "go all Newt Gingrich on me about this, I better know now." She had friends, her brother nearby and her mom a phone call away whenever needed. She could do this without a man, but needed to know, was he in for the long haul or not. And that night, holding her breasts, and only talking about how fierce Pat Benatar's vocals are, or what a passionate lyricist Patti Smith is, while silently letting her tears fall, Kim knew he was in, even once the scars would begin to set in.

•

A month before the surgery, Don decided to treat her to a night at the Hollywood Bowl. But Kim was tired. And crabby. The seats were too far from the stage. The people next to them kept staring at her latest wig. The symphony's wind section seemed off and they played all the wrong pieces. Even as Kim whispered these key points to Don, she knew she wasn't whispering as quietly as she planned. But she could not stop. And Don just kept nodding, and smiling at her, and holding her hand, sighing at times, but not saying a word to argue.

But the drive home was a different story. Suddenly, traffic caused Don to slam on the brakes, the parking attendants couldn't direct a wind tunnel if they tried, the radio stations had obviously sold their souls to pop song Satan, and the detour onto the 101 wasn't clearly marked as he swerved too quickly onto the freeway.

"Does it have to be so hard to get on the damn freeway around here?"

"Jesus, Don, it's not like it's cancer or anything," Kim said.

"Fuck it, Kim, that can't be the answer to *everything* that ever goes wrong now!" Don snapped.

She opened her mouth but stopped. Waited until the 101 led them toward the downtown LA skyline, where her office was, where she knew how to handle things, and where she still had the right answers. The glow of the buildings helped suddenly, gave a lift to her spine, and even though she knew she shouldn't, under her breath she exhaled a snarky "But it is . . ." before leaning in to change the station.

•

It was Kim's brother who had shaved her head that May. The first few clumps had fallen out as expected, long red lines that crossed her brush and clogged the drain in her shower. But after a while it just seemed thin in weird places, would literally fall down her arm during meetings and was a constant reminder of, well, being sick. She went to her brother's house one morning, found the clippers in his bathroom cabinet, and brought them out to the kitchen where he was having his coffee.

"I'm done. Just shave it all off," she told him, holding the clippers up at him like a sword. Dexter hadn't seen her look so serious this whole time. Not since she told them. Not the few times he'd taken her to the chemo appointments. Not even when he sat with her while they explained to his daughter that Auntie Kim would be sick for a while but, before you know it, would be okay again, so please don't be scared.

"But it doesn't look bad, Kimmy. Maybe just wear scarves for a bit. It's still long and pretty."

"I don't give a fuck about pretty right now. There's a ton of it now, but this slow fade is taking too long. Before you know it, I'll look like some sad Christmas tree with a handful of icicles. I can't do it. Just please, shave it."

He looked at her and, for a second, thought she might be kidding. Thought she was playing one of her pranks, like she would when they were young. Like the time when he was 15 and she told him, all breathy and excited, that Julie Castro, the hottest girl at San Pedro High, was on the phone. And how, after she prepped him for thirty seconds on how best to sound smart and funny at the same time, and she handed him the phone, his heart pounding, she burst out laughing, saying over and over, "You should see your face right now!" But this wasn't that time. He reached his hand out, his heart was pounding, but she didn't burst out laughing. She simply put her hair into a ponytail, which he would later cut off and save in his desk for her, when she was ready to see it again.

•

"This is Kim Anderson. I'm returning Dr. Stewart's call."

"Of course, Ms. Anderson. I'll put you through."

Kim stared at the fountain at the base of her office building, distracting herself with the cross section of suits and skirts passing by, and the whir of construction around the corner. There were blossoms in the tree nearby, and though Kim knew they weren't really cherry blossoms, she decided that an early springtime in LA deserved cherry blossoms.

"Hi, Kim. This is Dr. Stewart. Do you have a few minutes?"

The call itself went fairly quickly. Words she half expected and heard, but didn't. Breast cancer. A very aggressive mass. Began in the ducts and spreading to the surrounding tissue. Chemotherapy. Surgery. Radiation. Family history. Mastectomy planned. Double mastectomy recommended. Prognosis good, likely twelve months total. One year. Back to 'normal' by next spring.

"I can send you all this via email, Kim. It will make it easier when you talk to your family. You'll need support and they'll want details. I can talk to them too, if that will help. You have resources. You're not alone."

"Yes, Dr. Stewart, I understand. And email sounds good, but I really should get back to work." Kim hung up her cell, walked back into the glass and metal lobby, smiled brightly at the security guard before entering the elevator and actually hummed along to the instrumental pop song that played the twenty stories up to her floor.

"David, don't forget to send that copy to me by the end of the day. Graphics needs to begin layout first thing in the morning if we're going to make that deadline."

And that's how that afternoon played out, Kim alternating between forwarding the right emails to the right coordinator, text to one, graphics to the next, keeping the production schedules running smoothly. And as each project got its proper parts, she followed by going downstairs to the fountain and calling her mother, then her brother, then her best friend, repeating the words again and again, telling who needed to be told, getting the timeline moving, getting her people in order, and planning the next twelve months in her head.

By four-thirty, after she told her boss, and after they discussed her medical leave and benefits, Kim was back at her desk, eyes glazed over the emails coming to her inbox. Her boss had told her to go home, but Kim wanted to get more work done, put the projects in order, and direct each part to its proper place as she could. She placed emails into folders and deleted those she knew she didn't need anymore. Then for a moment, Kim sat still, except for her hand, which hovered the cursor over the *Deleted* folder, swirling the mouse in tiny circles over and over again, enjoying the momentary sense of accomplishment.

WRITERS IN THE SKY

Bruce Gorden

Some stand erect and poised
white lumpy statues

Dare we see movement
from this anonymous Caballero
proudly mounted his battle steed
with one stony hoof elevated
mid-gait
a signifier of battle wounds

To the East
spanning a naked blue expanse
an approaching army
Thunder heads
Anvils and the rumbles
of distant hooves
retelling the power of Generalisimo Santa Ana
still later Guerreros
Villa, Zapata
and their Refugios al Sur
Insurgentes
Guerrero Negro

So much history
in the sky today
my son and I lying
on the grassy knoll
above the Presidio
overlooking Old Town
relating stories of Father Junipero Serra
credited for the founding of
the missions in California
and today Mission San Diego de Alcala
Tomorrow San Luis Rey

Unless, por su puesto
we are preempted by
more important historical battles
re-enacted in the San Diego sky

I WANT MY BEST FRIEND TO BE A POET

Bruce Gorden

I want my best friend to be a poet
so I told him put yourself on blab
and make sure every word gets down on paper

like when you described to me over the phone
antlers in velvet sticking up just a little higher than the grass
in your cherry orchard and the ears twitching
and you went on and on and I listened fascinated
about the cherries above and how fruit is really a
placenta for the seed and how much I really don't care
and listened in awe of you and how much detail you can pull
up out of your knowledge fund like the big rigs making
a run over the Grapevine down Bakersfield way
and the granny gear they used to make the first pull
up the windy backside of La Canada de Uvas while
the drivers either rode outside on the foot rail to
escape the heat generated by those big nasty loud
diesels, or walked along side for some exercise

and how much I thought you would love to read
how Walter McDonald describes the hardscrabble
Texas land he works and works and works where
dead stuff lays around waiting for scavengers
soaring higher than he flew those sorties in Viet Nam
to land and pick a living out from between the ribs
of a coyote or a calf that didn't quite make it back
to his momma's teat or how Gary Snyder would give you
California Lore 101 and 102 on an afternoon hike that may run into
the evening and then hear a graduate level discussion
of stuff I really don't give the rat's ass that appears in the droppings
of the fox we are investigating with stick in hand parting hair
and undigested debris and how I realize it is not your fault Gary
I don't love you and close the book I couldn't get through

and how, Brian, I hope you will become a poet and put yourself
on blab so I can learn what Gary and Walter could teach me
if I loved them like I love you.

TO LOTTA, I REMEMBER YOU

Cassady Lynch

I saw a picture
on a snowy television screen
of a girl with burnt copper
for eyes and I realised
the Made in Khimki doll I knew
who always sat on the red stool
next to the peeling metal door
was you.

I had lived
in Moscow for two months
when I first heard the сутенёр call
for your painted face
and I knew eyes green
as the Liffey back home
could never be Anna, but you
answered him.

One night
I watched as a white car
with dents and scrapes stopped
to let you in from the cold and I saw
the blue tulle of your skirt tear
through the closed door
as exhaust fumes choked
the July night.

The day I left
Russia behind for good,
the newscaster said your name
with a smile, like you weren't
a dead girl pulled from the Kanal,
or an eleven year-old missing
her home, just a story
to fill the space.

* Khimki is a small suburb outside of Moscow.
** сутенёр is Russian slang for pimp.

THE METER'S RUNNING

Richard Farrell

FOUR ERITREAN CAB DRIVERS UNFURL PRAYER mats along the slack river while I wait for Jamie in the parking lot. I know that they're Eritreans because of the words emblazoned on the sides of their orange taxis: Eritrean Cab Company. Where is Eritrea? How could there be enough Eritreans in Southern California to even form a company? They stand, then kneel and face what I presume to be Mecca, though for the life of me it seems like they are facing the wrong way.

In the passenger seat next to me, tucked inside a brown envelope, are five waivers.

Jamie arrives. She parks her black Lexus on the opposite side of the lot, taps a package of Marlboro Lights on the dash, and wiggles her fingers. The Eritreans wash air over their face and bend down on their rugs as she lifts a cigarette to her lips but doesn't light it. Last month, she told me she quit smoking. I guess we all hover around our good intentions.

Once a week we meet near this dying river. She pays, collects the waivers, and leaves. I don't know exactly who she works for, nor do I care. The waivers I smuggle out of my office are like bureaucratic permission slips, short cuts for people looking to save cash, or time, or hassle. And who isn't? Our transgressions, more or less, amount to a victimless crime. The money barely makes a dent in what I owe, but whenever Jamie approaches, I always feel a little thrill.

"Freddy," she says, opening the passenger door. She calls me this even though my name is Will.

Jamie is tall and thin, with perky breasts and a killer ass, which she twists into the seat as she slips me a brown envelope with five crisp hundreds inside. I pass her back an almost identical envelope filled with the waivers. But today, something seems different about her.

"They want Thirties, Freddy," she says.

"Forget it," I say. "I can't get those and you know it."

"Hey, I'm just the courier," Jamie says. She flips quickly through the waivers. "The offer would be five hundred per Thirty. Think about it."

"I've thought about it plenty. I'm not going to prison for this."

"The offer includes other incentives," Jamie says. She curls around in the seat and stares down at my lap. Her eyes grow darker and the tip of her tongue slides ever so slightly through her parted lips. "I could make a down payment right now."

She's always flirted with me, but never this directly before.

"No thanks," I say. I have no interest in complicating things with Jamie. What we do is safe now. Oral sex and Thirties up the ante. I love my girlfriend. I intend to marry her once I can quit my job and pay off some of my debts. Jamie shrugs her shoulders.

"Suit yourself. I'm just saying that I'm not opposed to an alternative arrangement. The offer is out there now."

She must've turned heads in her day, and she's still sexy, but she's approaching the end of her run. The makeup and clothes only help so much. Still, I'd be lying if I say I'm not tempted. But a blowjob isn't going to pay my bills.

"Look. The truth is this," she says stepping out of the car. "This isn't worth my time anymore. Either you step up to the plate and bring us the Thirties, or we'll be ending our little arrangement."

She strides back across the parking lot, her hips swaying as she moves past the Eritreans standing near their taxis with pearl colored prayer caps. They turn and watch her go, all of us mesmerized by her ass.

•

When I get back to my office, all I can think about are Jamie's offer and the Thirties. I'm like a man possessed, hell bent on his own destruction. The Thirties could solve my problems rapidly. And I've always preferred quick solutions to complex problems.

But I can't do it alone. I'm going have to convince my boss and silent partner, L.D.

Until six months ago, L.D. was a steady, honest bureaucrat. Then his wife fell ill and I brought him in on my scam. I'd been slipping a few forged waivers to Jamie for two years, but with L.D.'s help, I increased both the volume and quality of waivers. We clear two grand a month each, tax-free. He does it out of love and desperation. I just do it for the desperation.

When I get to his office, L.D. is on his phone. He motions me to sit down.

"Can't we increase the dosage?" he asks. "Well how much will that cost?"

I hate to say that his bad news bodes well for me, but it does.

L.D. played middle linebacker in college. On his desk is a grainy photograph, him making a tackle on a snowy field. But whatever fury once filled his youth has dried up. His curly hair domes back across his dark forehead and his unctuous face sweats even when the air conditioning vents frost over. He's too soft to be a manager and too soft to say no to me. There's no ferocity left.

"What now?" he says. He has a raspy, three-pack-a-day voice, but L.D. doesn't smoke. His only vice is knowing me.

"How would you like to kick it up a notch?" I ask. Clearly, things aren't going well for his wife. I feel almost guilty.

"Don't even mention the Thirties. I've told you ten times."

"They'll triple the price," I say. "We keep the regular deal in place, and throw a few Thirties at them. We could make a killing."

L.D. slumps back in his chair. His shoulders sag. With a crumpled napkin, he dabs the sweat on his forehead.

"We'll be smart," I say. "Get in, get out, and be done by Christmas."

"No fucking way," Persephone says that night after I tell her my plan. "You said you'd never go there. Willie Boy, you're in way over your head."

"So I don't know what I'm doing?"

"You're greedy," Persephone says. "You're stuck in a boring job pushing paper and you're looking for thrills. You're going to end up in jail, and I'm not a conjugal visit kind of gal."

"You don't know what you're talking about," I say.

Our cramped, one bedroom apartment smells of lemons and vanilla. My whole life has smelled better since Persephone moved in. And I've always been honest with her. She knows about the waivers. She doesn't approve, but she's never tried to stop me before.

"Don't do this, Willie," she says. "Use your big boy brain for once."

This sends me over the edge. I pick up the phone and dial Jamie's cell. I do it right in front of Persephone, and just to make my point clear, I don't speak in codes.

"I'll get you the Thirties," I say. I have no idea if it's even true. "But it's going to cost fifteen hundred per."

"What the fuck, Freddy?" Jamie says.

As I'm talking, Persephone unbuttons her shirt then slips it off. Then she slides out of her shoes and unhooks her bra. The line remains silent for a long time, while Persephone unbuttons her jeans. She's down to her panties when Jamie says, "Tomorrow, same place and time, shithead. We'll discuss it then."

Rather than joining me on the couch, Persephone turns away, closes the door and goes to bed. She knows just how to make a point.

•

The next day at the river, the Eritreans are praying again on their rugs. Orange cabs idle beneath queen palm trees and the dark men squat and kneel in various stages of prayer. The Pacific Ocean glistens just beyond a stone seawall at the mouth of this nearly defunct river. I tell myself to check the direction of Mecca. I tell myself that I should go to church with Persephone every once in a while. I tell myself that the Thirties will help.

"Twelve-five is the offer," Jamie says. "Take it or leave it. And don't talk about this over the phone, asshole. Don't you watch TV?"

"Does twelve-five include the other incentives?" I ask.

Without a word, Jamie reaches down and unzips my pants. She takes me in her mouth in the shade of a eucalyptus tree while the Eritreans pray.

Back at the office, I present the deal to L.D., who shakes his head then pounds his fist on the desk. The desk rattles and the floor shakes and I think he's going to leap and tackle me to the floor.

"You dumb boy," L.D. says. "You got yourself into this. You can get yourself out."

His shoulders load, his muscles clench. Linebacker L.D. returns. No more slouch, only fierceness, as if his fat cells convert to muscle before my eyes. The transformation is remarkable. It's also short lived.

"Look," I say. "I need the money. You do too. We're risking just as much with what we do now. "

"You're fired," L.D. says. "Pack up and get out. You're lucky I don't call the cops on you right now."

But I know he's in. I know that his anger and his righteousness are his last lines of defense. Otherwise, I'd be picking myself up off the floor.

•

When I get home that night, Persephone throws a jar of pickles at my head. I duck, wondering how she's found out so quickly about the blowjob. The jar grazes my hair, and then explodes against the kitchen wall. Green liquid sluices down to the yellow tile. Lumpy pickles and shards of glass litter the floor.

"You moron," Persephone says. She's calm but furious. "L.D. called. He was in tears."

I'm partially relieved that that the pickles missed and that Persephone doesn't know about Jamie, but I'm also stunned that L.D. would've called her. He's never met Persephone. As far as I know, I've never told him I have a girlfriend.

"His wife shits into a bag," Persephone says. "You've got him over a barrel and you don't care." One of the many great things about Persephone is that she takes the pain and suffering of strangers quite personally.

"We all have problems," I say.

"When did you become such a prick?" Persephone says. "When did that happen to you?"

It's a fair question and one I can't answer. I tell her that. I tell her that I don't like being so cold all the time. I tell her how I'm tired of people calling me dumb. But how do you fake emotion? How do you force yourself to feel something?

Another great thing about Persephone: honesty turns her on. The room smells of dill and we fall to the floor and make love.

"Everything is just a game to you," she says after sex. "When are you going to grow up?"

"Look ," I say. "I stamp and file paperwork all day. I'm a twenty-six year old bureaucrat with a mountain of debt. So I make a little cash on the side."

"Christ, Willie," Persephone says, "You have no idea what you're doing. You're going to get caught, my friend. And you're going to drag that poor man down with you."

"I'm not going to get caught," I say. "I do this for a while. I dig myself out and then I can quit that miserable job and marry you."

"What then?" Persephone asks.

"Anything," I say. "Maybe I'll drive a cab."

She laughs and nuzzles up into me and we both fall asleep. The next morning, she packs her bags and moves out.

●

L.D. agrees we can move three Thirties per week, but we can't push them in bulk. The Thirties will draw attention. This means I'll have to meet Jamie every other day at the river and pass one off at a time.

"It's in her pancreas," L.D. says flatly after we hash out the details. "She can't take it much longer."

"That's a tough nut," I say. I've never been good at these sorts of things. He's a desperate man. I can see it in his eyes, and I feel for him, I really do, but what the hell can I offer?

"I'm out after she's gone," he says. "You need to know that. And another thing. I'm not going to be much help to you, if things go south. I'm not strong anymore."

"We're not going to get caught," I say. "And you're as strong as an ox."

Later, I deliver the first Thirty. Jamie's wearing Spandex pants and her nipples jut out from beneath a tight white tank top. She walks right past the praying Eritreans and I remind myself again to check if they're facing the right direction. Jamie and I must be the living, breathing examples of why they pray so hard. She reaches for my zipper and I close the door. As the Eritreans pray a few yards away, Jamie's mouth wraps around me. I think how lucky they are, to be so disconnected from this world. Her mouth cages me tighter and I close my eyes.

"My girlfriend moved out," I say after she's done. She's holding the Thirty up to the light and checking its watermark. "She moved back with her sister."

"Stop," she says. "Save the confessions for your priest."

She hands me an envelope full of cash and we go our separate ways.

•

For two months it goes without a hitch. The money comes in quickly. I pay down my debts and start believing I can win Persephone back. Sure, I worry about things, mostly about getting caught. But it begins to feel normal. Even L.D. relaxes a bit.

Then one day, he fails to show up for work. I pace up and down in front of his office for half an hour before going back to my cubicle. At lunch, an email announces that his wife has died. Immediately, I call Persephone to tell her the news.

"Will you come to the funeral with me?" I ask.

"Like on a date?" she says. "You're one sick bastard, Willie Boy. What are you going to do now about your little setup?"

"I've got to get out of this," I say. "I can't take it any longer."

The next morning, Persephone shows up at my apartment dressed in black. It's been a while since I've seen her and she looks good, slimmer and sexier, as if that were possible. In spite of my pleading, we take separate cars to the church where a few dozen people have gathered. I'm the only one from the office. We sit toward the back and she prays silently on her knees. I'm turned on watching her pray. I realize how much I miss her, how much I want her back.

After it's over, L.D. shakes my hand on the church steps. He looks like he hasn't slept in a week.

"How you holding up?" I ask.

"I'm lost," he says. "She was my life."

Persephone hugs him and wipes tears from her eyes. Their embrace lasts a long time and she clasps his hand before she steps away.

In the parking lot, she asks me why they never had kids.

"Who?" I say.

"Your friend," she says. "L.D. and his wife. Don't you know anything about them?"

I practically beg her to go out with me again, and she must feel bad for me, or feel sad because of the funeral, because she agrees. We make plans to meet for dinner. Standing in the shadow of the church spire, she hugs me goodbye and I smell vanilla and lemons in her hair.

"How was the funeral?" Jamie asks at the river.

She is everything I don't want. She's redundant and vile and she only takes. She lacks—and this insight comes as something of shock to me—a soul. I suppose, if I'm leveling judgments, so do I.

"They want fourteen more Thirties by the end of the month," Jamie says. "The vacation is over."

"Give me a break," I say. "The guy's wife just died. What am I supposed to do?"

"Look, Freddy. Like I told you before, I'm just the middle man. I wouldn't piss these guys off though."

"Now you're threatening me?" But Jamie heads toward my lap without answering.

The next morning, I call in sick to the office and crawl back into bed. I wake at noon and find fourteen missed calls and a dozen increasingly angry messages from Jamie. I turn off the phone and go back to sleep. Around three, I wake up start getting ready for my date with Persephone. Everything else is of no consequence. She's all I want. I understand that now.

We go to an upscale Moroccan restaurant where she orders lamb kebab and tells me she's seeing someone.

"He's a law student," she says. "Third year."

"Jesus, the food isn't even out yet," I say. My stomach heaves.

"Willie, you need help," Persephone says. "I love you, but I let things go too long. You have to grow up."

"Don't do this," I say. "A law student? Seriously?"

She picks up the tab for dinner and tells me to take care of myself. For a moment, I think we're going to have sex, maybe in the back of her car, maybe back at my apartment, but Persephone closes her car door and drives off.

•

In the morning, one of the secretaries, young and quite pretty, stops me on the way into my office. I smile my most alluring smile at her, but she doesn't seem to notice.

"Did you hear?" she asks. "Lawrence is in the hospital. He tried to hang himself. That poor man."

"Who's Lawrence?" I ask.

"Mr. Dutton," she says. Her voice casts a shadow. "Your boss."

Then she tells me something else.

"There was a cop here," she says. "They came into his office and started asking questions."

"For a suicide attempt?"

L.D. coiled a bed sheet around his neck and tied it to rafter, but it snapped under his weight. He crushed his larynx, broke his arm, and lost vision in one eye. Poor bastard couldn't even kill himself properly.

I sit next to him at the hospital. I stay awhile, but he never opens his eyes. I don't know what I owe him, but I'm pretty sure he's better off than I am. His massive chest barely moves the covers up and down. I slip a thousand in cash beneath his sheet and leave to meet Jamie.

"That was a close call," she says. "What's he going to do?"

"He won't talk," I say. "Hell, he can't talk now. He wants to die."

"No hard feelings?" Jamie says with a grin.

"So that's it?" I ask. "We're done?"

She raises her eyebrows, indicating that I've just asked the dumbest question in the history of the English language.

"Tell me something," I say to her. "Do you ever wonder what it's all about?" She makes a sour face. "It wasn't supposed to be like this. I mean, did you really think this would be how life turns out?"

"Relax, Freddy. Now's not the time to be getting all philosophical."

"My name is Will," I say.

"Well, Will, would you like me to say goodbye properly?"

She smiles and leans forward, but I tell her no. She shakes her head in disgust, but she's dignified enough not to say anything as she leaves.

Outside my car, the Eritreans fold their prayer mats and tuck them away inside orange trunks. They stand around talking, laughing. A few light cigarettes. Then, one by one, they climb in their cabs and drive off, until only a single man remains, finishing the last puffs on his cigarette.

I walk over and ask if he's on duty. The cabbie looks puzzled, but he opens the back door. What's left of this river limps past in a muddy trickle. Gulls circle overhead. I notice, for the first time, that the day is beautiful. The man driving the cab has skin as dark as night.

"Where to, mister?" he says.

"Can I ask you something?" I say. "What's it like there?"

"Where's that, my friend?" he says.

"Eritrea," I say. "I imagine it's very beautiful. I've been thinking about it for a long time. What's it like there?"

"I'm from Cleveland, mister. I don't know where Eritrea even is," he says. Then he laughs, a most pleasant laugh, like he's been asked this question a thousand times before. "Where to, my friend? The meter's running."

CHARTING MY COURSE

Cheryl Latif

i have learned the language
of phlebotomy—
about butterfly needles,
how many breaths will take me
through a six-vial collection
& the art of waiting.

i have come to expect
the dispassionate demeanor
of specialists, the sound of starched
white coats, the chill of exam rooms.

sterile interpretations of antigens,
antinuclear antibodies & sed rates
have expanded my vocabulary
if not my horizons.

weather forecasts have become meaningless,
the shortest day of the year too long,
yet somehow days continue to begin
& end in rush-hour traffic outside my window.

absent reason, i travel hope.

TANGO

Cheryl Latif

past & future tango through the hours
of a father who soon won't know your name,
mother in stage-four reprieve.
this cadence of crises plays
in the background
like an old 45 on repeat.

in the quietude of morning, foghorns hold you
like bowed notes of violin & cello;
you stand mute within an opus
of memories. past & future tango by.
coda looms in the wings.

this year finds spring pushed aside
by an aging winter's arias of snow & ice.
these long nights at a cold window
evoke years syncopated by estrangement,
tempo of anger & silence, rest & repeat,
past & future's blithe tango through your lives.

soon the seasons will settle,
as did life between you.
you will say the things you need to say,
those things you've told yourself could lure
songbirds back to the garden.
those things that will let you
place an LP on the old turntable
& tango effortlessly into tomorrow.

A Day of the Dead Vignette

in six movements

David Schmidt

Beer Number 1.
The brass band plays *La Canción Mixteca*.

A man in a white hat sits in the corner of the yard, slouched over. As the brass band plays the first note of the song, he turns his head and eyes me suspiciously.

One elderly Mixtec farmer stands up from his white plastic chair, emblazoned with the "Tecate" logo, and begins to dance to the live music. His sandaled feet describe the simple waltz patterns of the chilena, a traditional shuffle in southern Mexican towns like this one. The rest of us sit in a circle, watching him. The campesino's hands are crossed behind his back. He kicks up a small cloud of dust in the middle of the dirt patio, drifting in and out of the doorway of the adobe house where several cases of beer are stored.

Policarpo, the host, raises his bottle of Victoria-brand beer. "Let's drink to the health of these lovely visitors!" he shouts, tipping his cowboy hat in the direction of Judy and me. He nods to Valentina and takes a swig from his bottle.

Valentina, an indigenous person of the Mixtec ethnicity, is a native daughter of this town. She brought Judy and me here.

Beer number 2.
The brass band plays *La Llorona*.

Policarpo leans in toward me as I uncap my second beer. "Your friend Judy is pretty," he tells me in the Mixtec language. "Put in a good word with her for me."

The brass band is playing an instrumental version of La Llorona, a song whose lyrics make allusion to the legend of a weeping ghost who wanders the earth crying for her dead children. Policarpo has hired the town's band to play for this celebration he's hosting in memory of his wife, who died three years ago while he was in prison. That was on the eve of the Day of the Dead. As soon as he got out of prison and returned to his hometown, Policarpo started scraping together enough money to host a fiesta in honor of his wife's memory.

I stare around me at the mountains that frame the narrow valley where the town of Santa María Natividad is nestled. The hills around us are teeming with wild marigold flowers, known in Mexico as cempaxúchitl: the Flower of the Dead. They sprout up all over Oaxaca in the autumn.

It's the last week of October, just a few days before the holy days when the spirits of the dead return to visit the living. Most of the families in Santa María Natividad have already set up altars in their homes, elaborate adornments of flowers, food, sacred icons, photographs of their deceased loved ones. Chayotes, candied sweet potatoes, prickly pears, mole, tamales, tortillas, bottles of tequila and mescal.

The brass band continues to play; the musicians are all grade school children who practice year round and play professionally across the State of Oaxaca. As they instrumentally play the second verse of La Llorona, I can hear the lyrics in my head. "No sé qué tienen las flores, llorona, las flores del camposanto . . ." This verse describes the beauty of the flowers that grow in the cemetery. "When the wind blows them," the lyrics go, "they seem to be dancing."

"David, ask her if she knows how to make tortillas," Policarpo tells me in Spanish.

"Pardon?"

"Your friend Judy. Ask her if she can make tortillas. I have no one to make my tortillas for me. I can barely cook, and I'm all alone." He winks at Judy.

Judy responds in gringo-accented Spanish, laughing. "I don't know how to make tortillas."

BEER NUMBER 3.
THE BRASS BAND PLAYS *LA GUADALUPANA DE TEPEYAC*.

We clink our glass beer bottles together. Policarpo teaches me a traditional toast in the Mixtec language; translated literally, it means "Drink, my brother, because I am drinking."

Policarpo's in-laws call everybody "brother," but never in the context of a toast. They don't drink at all—they're Fundamentalist Protestants. This, Policarpo tells me, is why he has not been able to host a party to honor of his wife's death until now, three years after she passed away. The Protestants don't believe in celebrating the Day of the Dead. This syncretistic holiday, along with alcohol, tobacco, dancing, and playing cards, is the work of the Devil.

"Those Fundamentalists don't respect their dead," Policarpo's brother Olegario tells me. "They just dump them into a hole without any ceremony, like a dog."

"I think it's sad that the Day of the Dead and its traditions are on the decline," I respond. "There's something beautiful about the idea of communing with those who have passed on."

The man in the white hat is still glaring at me from across the patio, and I wonder if he is one of the Fundamentalists who attribute this holiday to Satan.

"Some folks swear that if you check the bowls of mole and soup that are left on the altar during the week of the Day of the Dead, the food gets a little more sparse each day," Olegario tells me.

A dust devil blows by in the arid Oaxacan wind. Policarpo stares at it. Olegario walks into the house to bring us another round of beers.

BEER NUMBER 4.
THE BRASS BAND PLAYS *YO SOY UN FEO*.

An elderly woman sitting on a low wooden stool wraps her rebozo shawl more tightly around her arms and shudders as the dust devil blows past. She whispers something to Valentina in Mixtec.

"What was that?" I ask in Spanish.

"She says the dust devil is bad luck," Valentina translates. "Sometimes those remolinos carry evil spirits inside them."

The woman looks up at me as Policarpo uncaps my beer, and smiles. I ask Valentina if she knows how old the woman is. "Nobody's quite sure," Vale tells me, "but she's the oldest woman in town. She remembers the Mexican Revolution." Which would make the woman well over a hundred.

Vale asks the anciana in Spanish what she remembers from the Revolution. "Oh, I was just a little girl at the time," she replies in Mixtec. "My parents hid me in the cellar with my sisters when Zapata's troops marched through town. They had some gold coins that they hid in the cellar with us, too. They were afraid the rebels would steal their gold and their women."

The hills and adobe homes around us turn a dark shade of bronze as the sun lowers.

Policarpo looks back at Judy and grins. His gold tooth glimmers in the sunlight. "Are you sure you don't want to come live with me and make my tortillas for me?"

Judy and the ancient woman both laugh. The tone of Judy's laughter is an octave lower than the old woman's; their tandem voices frame the last notes of the band's song.

BEER NUMBER 5.
THE BRASS BAND PLAYS *LA MALAGUEÑA*.

"I'm so happy that I can finally commemorate my late wife's death." Policarpo waxes nostalgic. "And to be able to remember her in the company of such beautiful guests!" He toasts Judy and me.

"It's like her own family doesn't even care that she died," Olegario says. "Those Protestants don't believe in anything."

The ancient woman who witnessed the Revolution leans in to Valentina and whispers something. Valentina later explains to me that the woman said she saw two figures inside her house the previous night. They were standing in front of her altar to the dead, eating in silence. The door to her house was locked the entire night.

"We used to all follow the ancient ways," Policarpo tells me. "Then all these new churches started popping up. And all of them claim to be 'the one true Church,' and they all say that we Catholics are going to hell. Only two hundred people live in this town, but now we have a dozen different churches."

A visitor from a neighboring community, of the Triqui ethnicity, suddenly speaks up. "We don't have this problem where I come from," he says in belabored Spanish. "Some missionaries came to our town trying to divide our people, but my uncle chased them off with his machete." He chuckles. "Problem solved."

The machete story inspires me to ask Policarpo what life was like in prison. "Bonito," he responds. "Quite nice."

I'm surprised. "Bonito? No knife fights? No flaming mattresses? No shower rape?"

"I just kept to myself, and people left me alone," Policarpo says. "It was nice. We got three square meals a day and a bed to sleep on." He stands up and heads toward the house to bring us another beer.

I notice that the man with the white hat is still glaring at me. I wonder if it was a good idea to bring up the subject of Policarpo's time in prison.

Beer Number 6.
The brass band plays *En el Último Trago Nos Vamos*.

The man with the shifty eyes and white hat drinks his beer in one fell swoop, wipes his mouth with the back of his hand, and picks his machete up from the ground. He looks over at me and gives me a toothy smile.

The smell of wood fires mixes with the sweet aroma of dry brush. On the horizon, the sun winks farewell and dips down into the valley west of town, toward the river where ancient, sacred caves and haunted springs dot the Oaxacan countryside.

Policarpo gives Judy her beer before he gives one to me. "I told you, Policarpo," she says laughing, "I don't know how to make tortillas. You don't need to keep doting on me!"

"I don't care, I can make my own tortillas!" he confesses. "Marry me anyway!"

I glance back in the direction of the man in the white hat—and see that his face is suddenly inches from mine. His machete rests at his side. He's saying something to me in slurred Mixtec.

"What is he telling me?" I ask Valentina, trying to hide the concern in my voice.

I can feel the darkness of twilight closing in around me. The man's fingers close around the handle to his machete. The other men are silent. A cricket chirps.

Valentina smiles.

"He thinks you're his nephew," she says. "He has a nephew he hasn't seen in years, and he figures it must be you since his nephew had lighter skin."

The other men on Policarpo's patio all start to laugh. One of them whispers to me that they have been egging the man in the white hat on, assuring him that I am the long-lost relative. "Well, I suppose a specter nephew is better than no nephew at all, during the holidays," I say. "Let's take a photo together."

Judy pulls out her digital camera and stands up to photograph us. The last rays of sunlight extinguish behind her as my new "uncle" drapes an arm around me, beaming proudly for the camera. Right as the flash goes off, the brass band plays the last note of the song.

I turn to the man in the white hat. "Happy Day of the Dead," I tell him.

YELLOW STILETTOS

Karen Stromberg

won't salvage
a hopeless universe.

Their cruel beauty
requires the stuff of saints:
to suffer
and blame no one,
to suffer
and never complain.

Even the most advanced
anorexic
can't endure
the four-inch stab

of a fallen metatarsal,
or those hopelessly
gargoyled toes.

MORNING TRAIN
TO AUSCHWITZ

James McCollum

Darkness in the boxcar,
The train lurches forward.
We all fall back into each other.
People are crying, some are screaming.
My mother is sighing. The smells, I gag.
Sunlight flickers in and out now,
Keeping time with the clickity clack of
Steel wheels on steel track.
I look down at my shoes.
They are not new anymore.
The tarnished buckles
Peek through the pale yellow straw.

The Common Things We Do

Elizabeth Trude

Do not discount me.
Wide shouldered and open
Feet squarely planted –
I will listen
And wipe your mind
Of imagined darknesses.

Those things you think that
Make you cheap
And creepy –
I will show as only human
And valid of Redemption.

Sweet thing to me,
You are hardly alone or the first –
In you, there is nothing so awful
That has never been forgiven before.

Let me kiss you now
With nothing but love.
Let me hold your face
And smile the recognition
Of the common things we do.

INTO THE TWILIGHT

Laurie Richards

EMILY'S HAND QUIVERED WHEN SHE REACHED for the coffee pot. Her doctor had said, "Don't worry. You're in great shape at your age." She had winced at the clumsy compliment. He'd also said the tremors would be slight if she took a pill for her frisky thyroid. Frisky was her adjective; his had seventy more syllables.

Was she trembling because of her thyroid or her guilt? She hadn't told Joan about the move and dreaded the inevitable scene. Maybe the idea of the move itself caused the shaking. Sometimes, mostly at night when Emily lay in bed listening to her aged brownstone shudder, the idea of returning to Savannah after fifty years struck her as crazy.

Is this my version of a last fling? Or was the truth more chilling? Am I worried that death is closing the gap because I'm standing still?

She held the carafe toward Joan. "More coffee?"

Her daughter had arrived early enough for chitchat, but after they covered the news and Joan's busy schedule, their conversation wound down quickly, like a cheap music box. Joan glanced up as she held out her cup. "Did you take your pill, Mom?" she said and turned her attention back to the *Times*.

Joan visited more frequently these days. "Just to make sure you're getting along okay, Mom," she had said when the mother monitoring started.

Of course Emily was okay, although a year earlier, she'd made getting along easier by closing off rooms she no longer used. But, with the shrinkage of living space, she felt diminished, like a piece of plastic wrap that shrivels in on itself. During forty years in Brooklyn Heights, Emily had watched the area slip into senility, then roar back, galvanized by young professionals, but not by Joan, who lived in Cobble Hill. Emily had offered to let Joan turn the unused rooms into a separate unit for herself, but Joan opted to remain separated by at least a neighborhood.

Emily was thankful Joan had not tied herself down to daily hovering because Emily saw the visits for what they were. Early-stage role reversal. Long gone were the days when Joan would try a four-year old's trick to get her mom to stay home from work. Emily fixed on that image of little Joan at the front door, one hand on her hip and the other held out, offering up a pretend wound. "You gotta stay and fix it, Mama." Emily had scooped up her sad-eyed girl and kissed the 'injury' before unwinding Joan's arms as she set her down. She had fixed the pretend wound and ignored the real one, the one she couldn't fix because, after the divorce, she had to work. By age five, Joan stopped the tricks and settled for a long goodbye hug.

Emily hoped that the career-woman Joan, the Joan sharing coffee with her now, understood why her mom left for work all those years before. She peered at her daughter, taking in her full brows–the left one scarred from a fall on the soccer field in middle school–and her dark hair, showing tiny flecks of gray in the bangs. Was the four-year-old still there, hurt and hovering? Surely, childhood wounds make way for the business of living as an adult?

•

She set her cup down and stifled a sigh. Too soon, Joan would look middle-aged and experience menopause. Emily's biological clock had stopped ticking two decades earlier, the last tick unheralded at the time. In the beginning, release from the monthly inconvenience brought a new spring in her step. After a few years, different inconveniences arrived: her spreading hips, shrinking lips, and stubborn paunch, but the younger Emily—the one who twirled a baton in high school and breezed through college and the bar exam after all-night parties—was irrepressible.

She looked toward Joan, who was still shielded by the *Times*. "Yes, dear," Emily said, answering aloud the interrogation yet to come on this visit.

Joan lowered the paper enough to reveal her tilted head. "What, Mom?"

Emily merely smiled and slipped a sugar cube into her cup.

"You seeing Ruth today?" Joan said.

"I cancelled."

Joan squinted. "Why? You okay?"

•

With increasing frequency, Joan's concern translated into something like a deathwatch. You're seventy. You're ancient. You could drop dead any minute. Emily tried to appreciate her daughter's concern; it was marginally preferable to the invisibility she endured in the crowded streets of Brooklyn Heights. Maybe she'd always been invisible and simply too full of her own schedule to be aware of it. Or does the species turn its eyes away when a member no longer produces? Will she be just as invisible in Savannah?

I'll pretend it's because I'm a stranger in town, not because the world is separating from me.

Emily ran her finger around the cup's rim. She brought out her best Wedgewood for these visits, a delicate floral pattern selected in her youth. It was too dainty for a quick coffee, but it shouldn't only collect dust in the china cabinet.

Joan looked at her watch and stood. "Gotta go. Tell me again. Why aren't you meeting Ruth?"

Emily rose from the table, feeling that soreness in her hip. She resisted the urge to rub away the ache. "On good days, our conversation rises to the level of vitamin ads, but usually we stick to the topic of surprising body noises. Soon it'll be a competition for the first hip replacement."

Joan gulped her coffee. "So what will you do? Get some exercise, I hope."

Emily knew her report card needed an A in the "makes good use of her time" category. Several responses knocked around in her head.

Organize my underwear drawer. Read the obituaries. Masturbate.

Exactly when had she become the child and Joan the mom?

"I'll surf the net," she said, "and send some twitters."

Joan chuckled. "I think you mean tweets." Her grin turned serious too quickly. "Have you tried that Pilates DVD I gave you?"

•

Emily nodded as she reached for the goodbye hug. Lately, Joan had employed a brief and careful embrace, as though her mom's bones might splinter.

When the front door closed, Emily chided herself for her cowardice. One more day that she'd let silence take charge.

Only a month before, on the morning of her seventieth birthday, the first phone call was not a birthday message; it had been her property manager in Savannah.

"The tenants in your parents' house moved out sudden-like. Your daughter said you might want to sell when that happened. They left something of a mess." The list of their sins included a cracked mirror in what had been Emily's bedroom until she moved away after college. The mirror was older than Joan. Heck, the crack was older than Joan.

"You can't blame them for the mirror," Emily said. "I threw a brush."

There was a pause at the other end of the line. "You threw a brush?"

"Bad hair problem. Prom night." Then she told him, she knew not why, to hold off on any repairs.

After hanging up, she'd been drawn to the mirror above her dresser. She pinched the thin skin beneath her eyes, and it held together briefly even after she let it go. The whites of her eyes weren't as bright as they used to be. Was her nose wider? Her ears larger? Would that cracked mirror in Savannah be more kind?

Okay, she was old, but she didn't have to act old. She was infertile, but her life didn't have to be. She needed a complete change, and she would launch it in Savannah. The Plan became her new child, conceived at seventy. She hadn't told Joan because that would've been like taking a morning-after pill.

She listed her brownstone and primed The Plan for delivery. The only heaviness she felt was the burden of keeping it secret from her daughter. On each visit, Emily resolved to tell her, but, so far, she had remained sly, responding dutifully to her daughter's regular list of demands disguised as questions. "Have you read that brain fitness book I brought? I check my blood pressure every week, do you?"

Emily had told only half the truth about why she cancelled her usual Tuesday lunch with Ruth. True, their conversations no longer merited an expensive bottle of pinot grigio. Pale gold liquid swirling in crystal inspired Ruth to spew out a litany of consumer reports on adult diapers.

"We don't need them now, but we will," Ruth had said with a wink and her two years older-but-wiser look.

After that, Emily redoubled her efforts on the treadmill and twice increased the resistance level. Joan didn't have to worry. Emily was determined to keep her hips moving and her brain chugging away. She did her best thinking on the treadmill. That's where she hatched all details of The Plan.

Tell her, she had said to herself many times and each time imagined delivering the news. Always, she also imagined her daughter's reaction. Joan would hide her relief, but a flitting twitch, an inaudible sigh would turn to astonishment that Emily made a decision without consulting her, that her mother would move out of a suitable monitoring range.

The doorbell rang, bringing her back to the other reason she had canceled lunch with Ruth. She ushered in the real estate broker and showed him to the coffee table by the sofa. As he set out the documents, he complained about the volumes of waivers and required disclosures that needed her signature.

"I'll explain each one, Mrs. Mason."

"No need," she said. "I was a real estate lawyer."

The surprise on his face was its own disclosure. That's what she got for adding the brag. She'd never been that young, his look said. I'm still that young, she would have shouted if his opinion mattered. Instead she told him she'd call after she'd read and signed them. "Make it soon," he said. "The buyer's anxious to get everything tied down."

Before he left, he looked around the flat. "Need any help? With finding a mover? Calling utilities?"

She gave him a you-dear-child smile. "Thank you, but I can still punch numbers on a phone."

After he left, she emailed dinner invitations for Friday to her "Friends" address list, a dwindling group, what with two recent deaths.

Then she called Joan.

"Hi, Honey, it's me." She almost added, 'I'm fine.'

"You okay, Mom?"

"I was wondering. Can you pick up some of the Rondo's terrific cornbread for me on Friday. I'm giving a dinner."

"Well . . . sure."

"Enough for eight. You're welcome to join us, but be warned. You'd bring the average age down to sixty-five."

"I have to pass. Eric and I are going to Connecticut this weekend." Eric's name was mentioned more often now. He was a keeper, one of the reasons Emily had been able to think about moving. But did she really have to wait until Joan found someone?

Am I over-mothering her as much as she's over-mothering me?

"In my day," Emily said, "we didn't admit to our moms about spending weekends with a man."

"Much better, isn't it, that people don't have to sneak."

Should I tell her now?

Joan saved her from stepping off that cliff. "Sorry, Mom. Gotta dash."

Emily hung up with a shaking hand. Not a tremor. A coward's shake.

In my day. What had she meant by that anyway? That she once had a time, and now it was over? That she no longer claimed a place in the world between sunrise and sunset? What was left to her? Maybe just twilight—the gloaming. She loved that word. It sounded like a time of magic, a mysterious time wrapped in silk.

In my gloaming, I'll revel in Savannah.

•

On Friday, when Joan arrived, Emily was in the kitchen arranging a centerpiece with gold Gerberas and greens. Emily wore a Williams-Sonoma chef's apron over a silk black pants suit. Both had been birthday gifts from Joan.

"You look good, Mom," Joan said as she patted Emily's hip. "See. Pilates works."

She raised the Rondo package. "I brought a quart of that soup you like."

Emily smiled as though grateful.

The soup you want me to like.

She didn't say it aloud because, these days it seemed Joan's sense of humor evaporated at the brownstone's threshold.

•

"What do I smell?" Joan said.

"Roast chicken."

Joan lifted a lid from a pot on the stove and peered inside. Emily watched as she glanced into another pot. "Collard greens and okra, Mom? I didn't know you like them."

"I grew up on them." Emily cut the stem of a Gerbera and inserted it into the arrangement.

"What's for dessert?" Joan's voice had that slice of inquisition in it, the tone she used when she questioned why on earth her mother would do something different from the habits Joan considered safe.

Emily felt a pang. Guilt again. Joan had a right to be inquisitive. Her own mother's concealing something big.

"Peach cobbler for dessert," Emily said.

"Cornbread, collard greens, and cobbler. Okra. All very Southern. You sure the chicken isn't fried?"

In her daughter's mind, fried chicken would have been a nail in Emily's coffin. "I promise," Emily said. "But you're right. It's a Southern-style dinner." She turned the floral arrangement in a circle to view all its angles.

Joan touched a bloom and grinned. "Looks pretty. You could come out of retirement. Be a floral designer."

Emily picked up the last Gerbera. "Good idea," she said. "I'll open my own shop."

Joan's jaw dropped. "I'm just kidding, Mom."

•

Emily paused, the stem not yet inserted. "Well, so am I, Honey."

Joan squinted. She was wearing her hair drawn back in a bun. Emily hated the severity of that style, but Joan had dubbed it 'crisply professional.' "What're you up to, Mom?" she said. "Why this dinner? Why now?"

Tell her.

I'm moving to warmer climes and younger spirits. A quest for immortality.

Emily placed the flower in the centerpiece. "Do you have a minute?" she said and didn't wait for an answer before walking into the living room.

Joan followed and sat at the far edge of the sofa, her eyes darting toward the well-set dinner table. Emily fluffed a floral sofa pillow, a gesture calculated to hide her shaking hands. She was still fluffing when Joan spoke.

"Out with it, Mom."

"I'm moving into my parents' house," Emily said.

Joan straightened, her posture as rigid as her hairstyle. "In Savannah?"

"Well, I haven't moved their house to another city." Emily immediately regretted the sarcasm. She stared straight into her daughter's eyes. "Right, sweetie. Savannah."

Joan was the first to glance away. She picked at lint on her skirt and deposited it on the sofa's arm. "You said you'd sell it after the renters moved out."

Emily stiffened. "When you suggested it, I said I'd think about it, and I did. But I'm selling this place instead. I've already got a buyer."

Joan huffed before she stuck out her lower lip. The wrinkle above her nose appeared. "You never even had a for sale sign. Were you hiding it from me, Mother?"

Oh no. Mother.

"I was afraid you'd try to talk me out of it."

I was afraid you'd tell me I'm too old, that I ought to behave old and stay put, disappear slowly, one spoonful of vegetable soup at a time.

•

Joan rubbed at the childhood scar, then reverted to a gesture of combing her bangs. "You don't know anyone in Savannah anymore." Her voice had turned desperate, confused. She waved a hand toward the table set for a proper sendoff. The delicate Wedgewood, too-ornate silver, and fragile Baccarat. "That's what this is all about?" Joan said. "A farewell to all your friends?"

Emily leaned back into the cushions, picturing herself as wisteria woven into the chintz. "There was a time I would've had to rent a hall."

"How can you do this to me, Mother?"

The question startled Emily. In all her weeks of scripting this conversation, she had not figured that Joan would see the move as something done to her. She reached for her daughter's hand and held it. Mom comforting daughter. "I'm not doing it to you, Sweetie. I'm doing it for both of us."

Joan drew away. "Hardly for me. If you need help, if you get . . ." She didn't speak the unspeakable. "How would I arrange care for you long distance?"

Emily surprised herself at how quickly a response came. "Remember last spring? Before you met Eric. When your company wanted you to transfer to London. Why didn't you?"

Joan stared at her. "That's not the point."

"It's a point."

Joan stood and paced in front of the coffee table. Three steps. About face. Three steps, about face. "I stayed in New York to be with you, Mother," she said.

"Sweetie," Emily said, "Savannah's not another planet."

"But, you're a New Yorker now, not a Southern belle."

Almost the exact words Ruth had used at their last lunch. Even Emily's doctor had opened his eyes wide at the news. "You can't go home again," they had both said. Emily had shrugged off the fear that leered at her whenever the facts were stated so baldly.

She stiffened her jaw. "Right," she said. "A complete change."

Joan folded her arms across her chest and planted her feet firmly on the carpet. "You're leaving me," she said.

•

Emily wouldn't mention how many times Joan had left her. College and graduate school in California. Jobs in Dallas and Chicago. Even after the divorce, when Emily was alone. No complaints. That had been the natural order.

Emily shook her head. "I'm not leaving you, I'm releasing you," she said. "I don't want to become completely dependent on you. I don't want you and Eric to spend weekends bringing me hot soup or analyzing *Consumer Reports* on nursing homes."

She moved forward on the sofa, regretting that she had leaned back so far. These days, the stiffness in her hips made getting up a four-step process. Scoot forward, brace herself, push up, step out. Joan offered a hand, which Emily ignored.

"I haven't minded helping you," Joan said. "But you need to remember you're not twenty anymore. Change is harder as you get older."

Emily looked into the dining area where the sale documents lay on the china cabinet. "These days, change is a sword swinging over me. The more scared I am to make this move, the more I have to do it."

Joan buried her face in her hands. Emily's own tears came, and she wiped them with an edge of her apron. She wanted the four-year-old arms around her again.

Joan's words puffed out through heavy breaths. "I just don't see how, at your age."

A strand of hair had escaped Joan's bun, and Emily tucked it back in. They reached for each other. Emily whispered in Joan's ear. "I'll come back whenever you need me, Honey."

"Why leave at all, Mama?"

Emily quivered at the word. She glanced toward the china cabinet. She could relent. She could tear up those documents. She could resume her regular lunches with Ruth and, when the time came, scour testimonials for adult diapers.

Joan hugged her tighter. "Why, Mama?"

Emily took a deep breath, leaned back, and touched her daughter's chin. "Because I still can."

PARIS LIES NAKED

Rebecca Romani

Paris lies naked
Under my skin
Just below the surface
ruffling pages of words.
Muddying waters
Opening windows
Slyly replacing English phrases, pale and fragile
With something more urgent, deeper than the breath we exchange
When we kiss
Je tiens à toi
Ca m'arrache le coeur à te quitter
I whisper to you in a tongue that runs through me
North and South
East and West
Un monde francophone
Under your English-speaking hands
Round vowels
qui s'inclinent la tête devant
sharp-edged consonants
Ô, mon âme,
Ca me déchire le coeur
A savoir
That soon, soon
I must leave you
As I left Paris.
As Paris
Left me.

HOLD MY HAND, DAD

Lanae Wangler

Are you proud of me, Dad?
Are you glad I was born?

I never thought that age could take you.
That time could cause your land to evaporate into tears
Turn the White House into mice
Your sweat into blame and bitterness
Thanksgiving aroma into mold
Yet keep the orange carpet fluffy and new.

As you watched the hail destroy the crops
The tornadoes approach from The West
The sun steal life from your fields of wheat
The clouds morph into dark enemies
You turned to Holy Water, time after time
And sprinkled it into the air.

Your golden leather shoes always laced around your ankles
Gave you the power and strength of a marching soldier,
An undefeated soldier.
I saw the dust caked on your lips and face.

I watched you dance, Dad, every polka and waltz
To celebrate your 40 years of marriage
I watched you dance only three, just now.

Your shoes are worn and so tired now, Dad.

Twenty-five years ago I hugged you for the first time
I felt your body stiffen, then freeze.
Your fists tight in your pockets.

Over time, the icicles began to melt through the cracks in your face.
The cold droplets helped you to raise your arms.
Over time, you learned to hug me back
You even learned to add a kiss.

When you're ready, hold my hand, Dad.
I will keep leading you
Until you are safely Home.

Agape

Joan Gerstein

"What would you die for?" the saint asks.
No hesitation, I whisper, "My son."
Only a parent can understand
the experience of absolute love
which engulfs a mother upon welcoming
her child, an eternal emotion that never
wavers, stays strong as granite, grows
with each moment of connection.

His suffering, a mother's pain, his hurt,
a mother's wound, success, a mother's joy.
A love so fierce you want to do battle
with his now and future enemies,

A child leaves your home, never your heart.
The signals from the center of your world
are faint and often fade away. He is your core,
but you are in his peripheral vision.
He's busy, remote, uncommunicative.
There is nothing you can do to ease the ache,
a phantom limb of what made you whole.
Distance does not diminish devotion.

FIREFLY NIGHTS

Laurie Richards

Y OU LOVE THE HOT, NIGHT BREEZE that whiffles through hollyhocks and rustles in sweet-smelling lilac bushes like a curious squirrel. The day's heat lingers, and the damp hangs heavy on your shorts and blouse that might have come straight from your mom's wringer washer in the basement. The moon's hiding somewhere. But you hope it'll come out soon because you like to talk to the glowing circle. Firefly lights flicker, and crickets chirp nearby, like they're saying, "the whole family's having fun."

Off you go down the alley to find your dad. "It's pay day" is all your mom says when you ask. One pay day you walked to meet him coming home from where he picked up money after hanging siding on houses all week, and he took you to Thompson's and bought you a cream soda and held your hand as you walked.

Your mom didn't cry when he came home that night and dropped money into her hand. "For rent and food and a little something for the kid," he said, and she smiled and winked at you.

But tonight you need to find him quick because it's already dark and maybe he stopped at a tavern, maybe the Big Pep, at the other end of the alley. He'll be standing inside with a lot of men, his elbows on the counter, one foot resting on a wooden rail and smelling like he's washed himself in beer, and he'll be slurring his words and he won't stop at Thompson's with you and he won't have money for your mom.

You make your way to the Big Pep with the help of lighted windows that line the rock-strewn alley like a connect-the-dots path. At Suzie's kitchen window, you see her mom and dad playing cards with other people. Her dad shouts "Ha," and you know he dropped the black queen on someone right then, and that his cheeks are shaking because he enjoys winning. On other nights, you saw his cheeks wiggle as he raised the card high and slammed it down. That's the kind of player he is, like your dad–a quiet man who turns into a pouncing tomcat when he dumps that mean queen on someone.

You duck as you pass their window because if Suzie's mom finds out that you're the kid making the rocks crunch, she'll yell, "Hey, Janie, does your mom know you're out so late alone?"

You come to another window with a light reaching out to the dark, and you're far enough away that you don't hear the bugs flinging themselves against the bare bulb, but you know they are because you hear it every night in your house, and it's a sound that stays with you, that popping sound like bacon frying.

The pebbled alley scrapes your shoeless feet, and you're glad. You want your feet barefoot-running tough, but it's early summer, and the city dumped new gravel in the alley, and it still feels sharp. The wheels of garbage trucks will soon wear down the gravel. By July, callouses will cover your soles, and the gravel won't hurt much when it digs into the spot near your big toe, although your feet are still tender tonight, and you wince with each step.

But you have a plan.

When you reach the Big Pep, you'll look inside, and if someone catches you sneak-peeking at the men crowded against the bar, they'll laugh and elbow your dad. Then he'll stagger outside, wiping away the foam from his upper lip as if your nose is too dumb to sniff out his beer and peanut breath.

"Go on home, Janie," he might say, but maybe it'll be early enough so that he won't be slurring his words and in his mean mood. Maybe you can coax him, and he'll be embarrassed in front of the other men, and then he'll take you to Thompson's and walk with you, and your mom can stop worrying that he'll spend all his money before he steps one foot inside his own home.

Anyway, that's your plan.

The fans set inside the screen doors of the Big Pep make a racket, not doing much good because the air is so laden with heat you could weigh it like your mom weighs the catfish your dad brings home on Saturdays. The Pep is crowded, but you can see your dad isn't there. He must be at the Blue

Waters Tavern near where he got his pay and that's too far for you to go alone. It's your mom's job to pull him away from there.

You make your way home, not through the alley this time because your feet are sore. You run past the television repair shop on the corner, then the funeral home, where you catch a whiff of lilacs, and the flickering lights of gray souls that pretend they're fireflies.

Your mom is in the kitchen. She sips her red Kool-Aid and swats at flies as you tell her about the Big Pep.

"You're coming with me," she says and takes your hand and holds your fingers hard and marches several blocks uphill, and it's dark, except for lights in houses you pass and dull street lamps on corners. The sidewalk is cool against your feet, and you skip to keep up with her until you reach the Blue Waters. They should name the place the Blue Stink because it always smells bad with cigarette smoke and beer, but the neon sign says "Blue Waters" in flashing orange and white, and tonight you don't wonder why they used orange letters for a blue name because your fingers are sorely squeezed in your mom's hand.

None of the men at the bar say hi or look at you or your mom. You both stop at the stool where your dad sits with a bottle of beer in front of him. When he turns around, he curls up his nose like someone is twisting it, like he sometimes twists yours, calling you a scamp when he's feeling good, except if he's in a bad mood, it hurts when he twists it.

Your mom sticks her hand in front of him with her fingers spread out. He looks away. Then he glances at you, and you sniff as though you hate the smells, and he shrugs when you cover your nose.

Your mom's jaw tightens, and she says, in a loud voice as if she doesn't care who hears, "We need groceries, and the rent's late."

His mouth turns down and he drops crumpled money and coins into her hand. She shuts it tight and says to him, "You coming?" He turns back to the bar and picks up his bottle of Pabst Blue Ribbon and takes a long swallow.

Your mom tugs on your hand, and after you walk outside, she stops to count the money, and it must not be enough because, on the way home, she cries and lets go of you to wipe at her eyes.

She walks fast again, and even though the sidewalk is smooth, you stub your big toe as you run to keep up. Birds make a racket, sounding mad because you and your mom are passing by. You walk near lilac bushes, but you don't smell the blossoms because the beer air from the tavern still clings to the clothes that are sticking to your skin. You pass an alley lined with hollyhocks, like the ones near your house, but there are no rummaging sounds, no cricket fiddlings. No firefly lights.

The moon's out. Its face is full and glowing in the dark sky, and it's ready to talk. But you don't ask the questions tumbling inside. When it's behind the clouds, is it hiding in a hollow in the sky? When it's hiding, does it still see you? Does it miss you like you miss it?

DAUGHTER

Sherrin Sen

You are not disgusting
you are not yucky and icky
your palms are covered with the sweetest elixir
dripping with delight
sticky
rubbing into my hair, tangles
so overwhelmed with love
I do not care
you hurl those arms around my neck
so tight
that I cannot breathe
Though my lungs inhale, clearer fuller than before
big luminous eyes like mine
but full
replete with mischief, laughter
knowing only today
no murky marks
or gray tomorrow's
clear bright lines
like crayons
scribbled on my walls
but these I cannot take off.

DIGITAL

Brian Thedell

At first you're not even there, but then
suddenly you rise, swell until
the air above fills itself with your hum and heat;

You draw yourself into a perfect wave
—unbroken—
like the hills that bob and weave on the kitchen window's horizon;

Yet I am like television static, like
billions of bits broken again into bits
or like the fog as it engulfs the morning hills, or something else . . .

In my breath, my vapor, I sound out the letters of your name;
I'm in love with all the little parts I can't seem to split;
enchanted, I follow you, like a dog's eagerness.

And so yes, my dear, we strange quantum opposites
fashion together a common tune, a common tone;
we harmonize between the La-Z-Boys and the entertainment center.

This Saturday at dawn I'll hike that horizon's summit,
and as the sunrise-golden dirt plods beneath my feet I'll remember
the little bits, the pebbles, the blades of grass:

they compose that perfect, rolling hill;
they weave an image—a bitmap, a jpeg—
a dusty haze of my love for you.

THE QUANTUM MECHANICS OF FALLING IN LOVE

Jessica Broughton

D APHNIS CRAWLED INTO THE SAFETY OF HER BED and turned out the lights. As soon as she drifted off, her molecules began their nightly ritual of quantum drift, like surf-washed sand on the cosmic ocean. Her electrons increased their spin, humming and vibrating until the forces that bound her together were broken. Her body dissolved in an instant as an unseen weaver unraveled her, bit by bit. She became nothing and everything all at once. The soft blanket that had so recently caressed her tired limbs billowed onto the empty bed as if she had never lain there at all. She would be there in the morning, just as she was every morning, when her unnatural nightly rhythms determined she was ready to become her physical self again.

As she became the bits of star stuff she wondered, in her mind without a mind: "Is this what happened to Buddha when he sought enlightenment? Did he forsake everything that made him human?" That would have meant to forsake love, too, and love was all she felt—overwhelming, unconditional, true love for Alonso. There were no expectations, no day-to-day complications, and their whole relationship existed outside the plane of reality, and yet it was the most real thing she had ever known. Her physical body remembered his as they danced wildly together on their nocturnal sojourns. Daphnis could feel the heat on her skin when she rematerialized the next morning as though their bodies had touched.

In this alternative plane of existence, life was whatever they wanted it to be. On this night in particular she chose the beach for their intended rendezvous: a clear pristine shore with tar black sands and a purple moon that seemed to dance across a scarlet sky in an erratic orbit. She assembled her dissolved particles and sat on the beach and waited. She waited as she had for the past three months knowing Alonso would not meet her. Their time together had been sporadic at best since he started working at the Large Hadron Collider in Switzerland to discover the cause of their "condition," being the dutiful student of physics that he was.

Daphnis wanted to hate him for leaving her when they had spent every night together like this since they were children. She just couldn't hate the only person in the universe who truly understood her. She remembered Alonso telling her about Niels Bohr and his principle of complementarity, which meant they were both particles and solids, like beams of light, but they could only be observed as one thing at a time. The simple act of observing interrupted the natural state of being many things at once, which is why during the millisecond they were observed, or expected to be observed, they rematerialized. Alonso quoted Bohr: "The opposite of a true statement is a false statement, but the opposite of a profound truth is usually another profound truth." He told her his profound truth was that he loved her and he always would. He plucked out one of her atoms and placed it in the swirling mass of his own, giving her an atom of his in return. Alonso said this way they would always be together, no matter what happened.

That telling seemed innocuous at the time, and in the three months since she had last seen him, now it seemed like a premonition. Why they fell apart every night was a mystery altogether, and Alonso was hard at work in his lab to determine the cause of their quantum drift. It was the only chance that the two of them could be in the same space without causing a cataclysmic explosion, like when matter met antimatter. The last she had heard from him was a one line mysterious email: Daphnis, I've done it. Done what? He tried to explain his experiments to her and etched his equations into their beach to try and show her the mathematics that was always running through his waking brain. She tried to understand and to support his desire to understand, even if it was a desire she didn't share.

When she dissolved that night Alonso wasn't there. He had simply winked out of the existence of her life as quickly as he came. She watched the turquoise sea as the waves moved in and out in a rhythmic, rocking motion that was her only comfort. She felt as alone as she had when she first discovered that she was not like other children. It was the first day of kindergarten, a monumental day in everyone's life, and the day she learned she was different. Daphnis mustered up all her courage to say hello to the little girl at her table, and in her excitement asked what she did every night once her body came apart. The little girl moved her seat, told the teacher, and Daphnis' parents were called in because her "overactive imagination" frightened the other children. From that day forward she kept her secret to herself.

Until Alonso came along.

She met him a few months after she first experienced her nightly fizzing, as she called it. When she deatomized every night she thought it sounded like her mom pouring fizzy water in her juice glass. After spending her whole life fizzing most nights, she wondered if she could see something more than the infinite blackness. Even though she felt safe in the dark, it was boring. One night she thought maybe, just maybe, she could go somewhere. Looking at an encyclopedia in the school library, Daphnis found a picture of the Eiffel Tower and decided she wanted to see it. After her parents kissed her goodnight and snuggled her into bed, she pulled the encyclopedia out of her backpack, jumped back under the covers, and turned on her flashlight. She stared at the picture and thought about it and wished to see it with all her might, like making a wish before blowing out the candles on a birthday cake.

Now Daphnis thought back on her childhood comparisons with amusement at how naïve she and Alonso were. Because her wandering thoughts turned to their first meeting, the Eiffel Tower materialized in the middle of the beach. It was at the Eiffel Tower that she first saw him. Alonso was waiting at the bottom, sort of. She knew intuitively that he was there and he was a boy, and even though she was sure he was in the same state she was, she could see him—the black curled forelock, dark eyes, and pale skin made up his solid state. She was so grateful and relieved that there was someone else here she forgot her natural shyness and the world she was sure she had created.

"Hi!" Daphnis said, swirling her energy together to approximate a wave. If she had been there physically she would have smiled when he waved back, and yet, she knew this stranger knew she was smiling. Before she could stop herself, she blurted out, "Does this happen to you every night too? Do you visit here every night? How long have you been doing this? Where else have you been?"

"Yes," he said proudly. "I do this every night and I can go anywhere I want. I've never met anyone here before. Let's go to the top of the Tower. Watch how fast I can fly there!"

Before she could answer, they were whirling and flying and laughing.

By that time, awkward teenagers that they were, they also knew they had never really been to the Eiffel Tower but were visiting a world of their own creation. They just got lucky, very lucky, they thought of the same thing at the same time. She made a game of trying to calculate the odds that two people would be thinking about Paris at one instant in time. Daphnis gave up long before Alonso had found the answer. By then they were having too much fun creating a world of their own where they could meet and talk and laugh and just be. When Alonso started college and began to study physics, they sent each other letters—real, physical, handwritten letters from MIT to her home in Washington, D.C.—as reminders to each other that they were real. He wanted answers and concrete reasons for why they could do what they did while Daphnis was content regardless. He sent her his research and the results of his fruitless experiments where he tried to explain why night after night they fizzed into another world and toward each other. In one particularly bitter moment, he questioned the existence of God, saying if there was an omnipotent observer then surely His eyes should keep the two of them from unraveling. She had argued that their chance meeting was an indicator of a benevolent force at work because now they were not alone.

The Eiffel Tower, the black sand beach, the colorful sky, all shimmered and fell into blackness, and suddenly Daphnis was back in her own bed. Seamus, her lovable black lab, begged for breakfast with his big chocolaty eyes, thumping his tail wildly on her bed when he realized that his beloved owner was awake. She gave the dog a quick pat, yawned, and got up to take care of her morning routine. Another night in a sea of nights added up to three solitary months. She put on her smile for the world as she dressed and hoped her heartbreak didn't show. Seamus's wagging tail and jovial bark transformed her smile into a real one for a microsecond. She pushed the thoughts out of her mind—although she did allow herself the luxury of a malcontented sigh—fed Seamus, and made a fresh pot of coffee in her French press.

She sat down at her tiny kitchen table with her own breakfast and her laptop. The coffee was warm and fragrant, and as the vapors rose through her nostrils, they tickled her brain. Her first response was to move her eyes to her email—nothing. Then to the phone. The screen beeped at her petulantly when she pushed the buttons. No messages. She caught a glance at her wall calendar and saw just how many red "X's" there were. They ran across the paper, underneath a black and white photograph of the Eiffel Tower, scarlet chorus girls kicking up their legs and shouting "No!" with each successive mark. Daphnis placed another X in the box for yesterday's date. She turned her eyes away and glanced out the window, where it seemed the sky mimicked her dark mood.

Seamus wiggled his head underneath her hand, his not-so-subtle way of telling her if she was going to stare out the window she may as well do something useful. She took his big, floppy coal black Labrador ear between her fingers, and Seamus made happy grunts, lost in the pure joy of being petted. Daphnis was jealous. Alonso had imprinted himself on the very fabric of her being, and in losing Alonso she had irrevocably lost a part of herself. All she had now was the one molecule of his embedded in the billions of her own.

On days like today, cool drizzly autumn promised frost and hot chocolate right around the corner; these were the days when Daphnis missed Alonso the most, even if she couldn't share them with him in person. She pulled her wool pea coat around her and walked down the city street, passing by couple after couple clinging to each other in the chilly air and glowing as brightly as the dry leaves that crunched under their soles. She missed having someone to share the monotony of grocery shopping and the joy of a home-cooked meal, and she missed rummaging through random bookshelves in search of a good read with a partner in tow. She had been able to handle all the monotony of the day-to-day by herself as long as she had Alonso at night, and now it looked like he had disappeared forever.

She entered her favorite bookshop and smoothed her windblown hair. Sleigh bells clanged against the oak and glass door announcing her arrival. Daphnis paused, closed her eyes, and inhaled deeply. The scent of mold and old paper filled her nostrils and enveloped her. She quickly walked in between the stacks, taking care to avoid the shop's Snogging Corner, and made a beeline for the first editions. She lost herself in the touch, relishing in the feel of the soft and supple leather beneath her fingertips before an annoyed cough ripped her from her reverie.

"Miss, I won't remind you again. Do not touch."

Daphnis blushed and waved an apology to the older woman who was forever looking down her glasses and telling her not play with books she couldn't afford. She ducked into an aisle where the less-expensive leather bound volumes were arranged in neat rows—the gold filigree announcing the titles on their navy blue and hunter green and maroon spines with a regal flare—and willed the color out of her cheeks. She was out of the clerk's range of vision and could peruse them without being watched. She pulled down a copy of *20,000 Leagues Under the Sea*, flipped to a random page, and lost herself in the adventures of Captain Nemo and the Nautilus.

She was no more than a paragraph or two into the novel when a hand caressed her shoulder and startled her out of her reverie. Every bit of her began to vibrate and hum until she was trembling, her own skin tingling with the sense she had missed over the last few months. The hand was firm, warm, and gentle; she knew who it was without looking. She turned and found herself staring at the face she had seen every night since she was six, the face she had longed to see again for so many months. His hazel eyes and contagious smile did not hide the fact that he vibrated too, with what looked to be a combination of excitement and nerves.

"Daphnis," he said, as he touched her check and swirled a few particles off of her with each caress. She was unable to respond. Her breath grew shallow and rapid; her body shook despite her best intentions to keep her emotions under control and in check. One lone tear escaped, a liquid, shining diamond, and Alonso caught it in the small concave depression just below the knuckle on his thumb. The tear steadied, and as they stared into it, Daphnis could see everything. She could see infinity—she saw him as a small boy of no more than seven, at his grandparents' ocean side cottage as he ran through the red gate that led to their garden to the sand dunes below, his stocky tan legs carrying him as sure and steady as a mountain goat to the sea below. She saw him at eighteen, leaving for college, head held high and defiant as he picked up his duffel, turning only once to see his mother wipe away a tear and then resolutely walking down the driveway, his straight back and rigid shoulders masking his own sadness. Getting drunk in London and vomiting in the tube station all over a businessman in a designer suit who had the misfortune of choosing this night to work late. Daphnis at the Eiffel Tower. His first girlfriend, feeling the touch of her soft skin as his fingers traced ellipses along her shoulders while he explored her mouth and tasted the slight waxy taste of her lipstick. Then Daphnis as they danced on their cosmic beach. The universe expanded out into the vast blackness and contracted upon itself into the tiniest pinprick of light. In him she saw everything and nothing.

The moment ended, and the tear fell out of the pool in his thumb, the thumb that she finds perfect. She looked into his eyes and knew he saw her, all of her, every moment of her existence as surely as she had seen his, and the walls she had carefully constructed crumbled. Her breath caught as all the grief of the last three months poured out of her in streams of tears. He gently took Daphnis into his arms and held her, gently wiping away every tear that ran down her cheeks. Then he kissed her—a long, slow kiss charged with the promises of an infinite amount of lifetimes and choices. He was real, and, more importantly, he was here. Alonso buried his face in her hair and sighed. "I've missed you so much," he said as he held her. She ran her fingers through his curls, feeling him for the first time and knowing, without a doubt, she would never have to let him go ever again.

"How? How is this possible? Where have you been, Alonso?"

"I accidentally walked into the Collider when it was on. Turns out that was the solution the whole time. I haven't quite figured out the mechanics behind it yet, but now I can control when I fizz." He took her hand in his. "I can control when you fizz, too."

They walked hand in hand as Alonso led her to the front of the bookshop. Daphnis noticed their hands seemed to be two halves of the same mold, like two pieces of a puzzle falling perfectly into place. They were particles and waves all at once, and their two contradictory pictures of reality blended together to become all realities. The sleigh bells jingled as they walked out into the cold fall air, and the woman working the desk called out her thanks, encouraging them to come back again. As they waved their goodbyes, Daphnis and Alonso fizzed out of their everyday existence and into the life that awaited them.

ABOUT THE EDITORS

MICHAEL KLAM directs the Poetry & Art Series at the San Diego Art Institute's Museum of the Living Artist (MOLA) in Balboa Park. Ongoing since 2001, Poetry & Art features local and national writers and artists ranging from emerging poets to Pulitzer Prize winners. Michael co-created the Page to Canvas to Stage program for MOLA and the California Arts Council. The program brings established artists, writers, and performers to local classrooms to workshop with students and staff. Michael's freelance work includes articles and features for *San Diego CityBeat*, *San Diego Source / The Daily Transcript*, and *La Prensa San Diego*. His publisher is Puna Press. His book, *Emma and the Buddha Frog*, was a San Diego Book Awards poetry finalist. Michael lives in Ocean Beach with his wife, Jennifer, and three kids, Emma, Henry, and Anya.

ANTHONY BONDS is the author of *The Moonflower King* (Calypso Editions 2012). He has worked professionally as a publisher, editor, and book designer in San Diego since 2008. He lives and writes in San Diego with his wife Amanda and their newly adopted dog.

Read Anthony's monthly blog post on SDWI's Fresh Ink blog at www.sandiegowriters.org. Learn more by visiting his website at www.anthonybonds.com.

CONTRIBUTORS

CLAIRE HSU ACCOMANDO has written nonfiction most of her life but has now happily embraced poetry. *Love and Rutabaga* (St. Martin's Press) is a memoir. Her work has appeared in *Women in World History, The Christian Science Monitor, American History, Art Week, Atlanta Review, Mudfish, California Quarterly* and anthologies.

LENISE ANDRADE is a Los Angeles native with a degree in English from the University of Southern California. She moved to San Diego in 2007 and is the Development Director for WiLDCOAST, a binational conservation organization. She likes turtles, full moons, and Sundays on her patio writing stories like these.

SCOTT BARBOUR is an editor and writer in San Diego. He is a member of San Diego Writers, Ink, and a regular at Thursday Writers. His stories have appeared in *A Year in Ink, Vols. 3, 4,* and *5,* and in the anthology *Writings on the Wall.*

STEVE BEDLE is a San Diego native and former disciple of the Creative Writing Department at Grossmont College. He has taught English in Europe and Asia and is currently studying English Literature at the University of Glasgow in Scotland.

JESSICA M. BROUGHTON has been a freelance writer since 2006, and has written about everything from apple pie to zombies, but has yet to write about zombie apple pie. You can read her work at *The Drabblecast* and upcoming at *Tales to Terrify.* You can find out more at www.grrlwriter.com.

CAROLYN BUDD returned to San Diego from Seattle where she worked as an art and drama therapist and theatre director. Her poetry recently appeared in *The Far East: Everything Just As It Is*. Her poem, *The Journey Home*, was inspired by her adaptation of a photo novella on migrant farmworker nutrition.

AMANDA BYZAK, when she is not spending time in the fictional world of sirens and other creatures from the deep, spends most hours of her day being a mother and teacher to her wild five-year-old boy, Adam, and a wife to her gem of a husband, Aaron. She also cherishes the serenity of long runs and nature walks.

WILLIAM CASS has had forty-seven short stories accepted for publication by mostly smaller literary magazines and anthologies. He lives and works as an elementary principal in San Diego.

REBECCA CHAMAA has been writing short pieces including poetry for twenty years. She has been published in *Evangel*, *Christian Women Today* and *Transition*. She enjoys baking, upcycling old clothing, and walking. She shares a love of San Diego with her husband of fifteen years.

KATE CURRER is an attorney, stand up comic, and writer. Follow her on Twitter @KateCurrer, or katecurrer.tumblr.com.

ANNA DIMARTINO graduated from UC Santa Cruz with a BA in Studio Art. She is a writer, artist, educator and mother to two wonderfully creative children. Her most recent work, a tribute to her mother, is scheduled to be published in the second volume of the Cancer Poetry Project.

RICHARD FARRELL is the Nonfiction Editor at *upstreet* magazine, a Senior Contributing Editor at *Numéro Cinq* and a faculty member at the River Pretty Writers Workshops. His essay "Accidental Pugilism" received a Pushcart nomination. He has published at *Hunger Mountain*, *Numéro Cinq* and *A Year in Ink, Vol. 5*.

JOAN GERSTEIN has been writing poetry since elementary school, but it has only been since retirement as an educator and psychotherapist that she has had time to hone her craft.

BRUCE GORDEN is a native of San Diego and a life-long surfer. He believes his first career as a Family Therapist was really a gathering of material for his true calling as a poet. He has heard many life stories from people who find a way into his writing. His Muse does not keep regular hours, so you might find him sitting on a curb or bus stop scribbling something he just received.

JILL G. HALL is a past board president of San Diego Writers, Ink, and former Brown Bag prompter. She has just completed the jillionth draft of her first novel, *The Black Velvet Coat*. She spends as much time as possible on her ranch in Descanso, where she finds inspiration and revitalization. More of her works can be found at www.jillghall.com.

KATHI HANSEN is a former trial lawyer whose work appears (or is forthcoming) in *The Rusty Nail, Literary Mama,* the anthology *Mad Road, Foundling Review* and *Per Cortra.* Kathi is currently working on a collection of short stories and a novel. She lives in Coronado with her husband and labradoodle.

LINDA HUTCHISON is a freelance writer living in La Jolla and the author of two books for high school students, *Lebanon* and *Finland.* Her poems have appeared in several journals, including *A Year in Ink, Vols. 1* and *5, Magee Park Poets Anthology,* and *The San Diego Poetry Annual.* She blogs at www.headwindjournal.com.

EBER LAMBERT has hosted the New Poetic Brew open mic and helped produce San Diego DimeStories for over five years. In addition to being the slowest carpenter on earth, he is currently compiling a collection of his short fiction and essays as a new way to avoid working on his albatross of a novel.

CHERYL LATIF was active in San Diego's poetry community until moving to the Northwest. Her poems have appeared in regional and national journals and anthologies. Her manuscript, *the longing of unrealized blossoms* (then titled *body language*), was a semifinalist in The Word Works 2012 national contest. Find her at www.latifpoet.com.

CASSADY LYNCH is an aspiring tweed-coated academic with a love of warm whiskey on cold nights. Her work has been published in *The Far East: Everything Just As It Is*. She will be completing an A.A. in Creative Writing in Spring 2013 and transferring to SDSU in the Fall.

JAMES M. McCOLLUM is a member of San Diego Writers, Ink, and also a retired airline pilot. He flew medical evacuation helicopters in Vietnam in 1968 and 1969. His poetry has been published in literary magazines and he has been invited to read his poetry at schools, bookstores, book clubs, and the Solana Beach Public Library.

Kelly Metz-Matthews is a copywriter and editor. Her most recent work, a collection of creative nonfiction, was published in 2012. Kelly lives in Oceanside with her husband, two precocious young children, and a nearly insatiable desire to read every book in her path.

REGINA MORIN is a long-time resident of Ocean Beach. An original member of the Border Voices Poetry Project, her poems have appeared in *Visions Magazine, America, No-Street Poet's Voice, San Diego City College Anthology,* the *San Diego Writer's Monthly, McGee Park Poets Anthology, A Year in Ink, San Diego Poetry Annual,* and *The Reader*.

LAURIE RICHARDS leads writing workshops for the CSUSM Extended Learning Institute and the Pasadena Library. Her work has appeared online and in the 2011 *She Writes Anthology*. She organizes the San Diego Book Awards Write to Win Workshops and serves as Judging Chair for the SDBA Short Story Competition.

REBECCA ROMANI is a local freelance journalist who teaches ESL and film for various universities. Her work has appeared in various publications such as the *Christian Science Monitor*, *The Levantine Review* and IPS.org. She is currently at large in Southern California.

RON SALISBURY has integrated poetry with business life for decades. Now, three wives deep, four children long, and assorted careers past, he continues to write in San Diego. Publications include: *Eclipse*, *The Cape Reader*, *Serving House Journal*, *The San Diego Reader*, *Alaska Quarterly Review*. His work was nominated for a Pushcart Prize, Honorable Mention, and City Beat 101.

DAVID J. SCHMIDT is a freelance writer, folklore researcher, multi-lingual translator, and home brewer in San Diego. He speaks eight languages and has published in English and Spanish. In addition to co-authoring the *Daily Book of Art* and *The Daily Book of Photography*, he wrote the erotica-romance parody, *Pirates of the Danube: the Erotic Adventures of Pepper MacOralby*.

SHERRIN SEN is working on her first collection of poetry. She is an abstract painter and writer. Hailing from Pakistan but raised in London, she lived and worked in New York City. She addresses issues of change, identity, and perception and celebrates the most unassuming moments in life.

CATE SHEPHERD is a psychotherapist and teacher in private practice, and author of *Emotional Orphans: Healing Our Throwaway Children*, which tells the stories of emotionally disturbed kids who healed themselves despite overwhelming obstacles. For over twenty years, she has specialized in the treatment of trauma through the power of understanding.

KAREN STROMBERG writes poetry and short fiction. She has a MA in Creative Writing—Fiction, two Pushcart Prize nominations and a "Statement of Accomplishment" from Coursera's highly recommended "Modern and Contemporary American Poetry."

Brian Thedell, shiftless ne'er-do-well, poet, and photographer, publishes most of his poems online at www.brianthedell.com.

Olivia Tomkinson is a member of San Diego Writers, Ink. She enjoys creative writing as an outlet to her professional role as a technical writer. She is currently working on various writing pursuits and is thrilled to make her debut as a published creative writer in this anthology.

Elizabeth Trude retired from teaching high school English a few years back to pursue the world of intrigue that is housewifery. Tending towards impulse and passion, she began homeschooling her three young children (not for creepy religious reasons). She wants to assure everyone that her children are well socialized and she is more than qualified with a BA in English and a MA in Education. This is her second appearance in SDWI's anthology.

Lanae Wangler, MA, began her educational career in 1998. She taught in the department Rhetoric & Writing Studies as an intern for San Diego State University, and she facilitated workshops for new teachers. She currently teaches English at the San Diego Met High School. She won Teacher of the Year in May 2012.

Gary Winters is the author of *The Deer Dancer*, winner of awards from: UC Irvine; San Diego Book Awards; Mensa Creative Awards; 2011 Book of the Year, and *ForeWord Reviews Magazine*. *The Deer Dancer* is in the curriculum at Southwestern College in the departments of Language, Literature, English, and Education.

ABOUT
SAN DIEGO WRITERS, INK

San Diego Writers, Ink, serves as a hub for the literary community, promotes literature, provides artistic development for writers at all levels, and facilitates artistic collaboration. The Ink Spot is home to the Ink Spot Gallery as well as the Ink Spot Press.

Having resided happily in the Art Center Lofts of the East Village for many years, the Ink Spot will soon be moving to a new home at Liberty Station in Point Loma. Naval Training Center at Liberty Station represents a phase of growth for SDWI within NTC's arts community. By August 2013 you can find us there, but until we move our location and post office box remain the same.

San Diego Writers, Ink   The Ink Spot
P.O. Box 34374   710 13th St., Studio 210
San Diego, CA 92163   San Diego, CA 92101
www.SanDiegoWriters.org

Past publications of *A Year in Ink* are available at our website.
A Year in Ink, Vol. 1 (2008), edited by Thomas Larson
A Year in Ink, Vol. 2 (2009), edited by Sandra Alcosser and Arthur Salm
A Year in Ink, Vol. 3 (2010), edited by Roger Aplon and Jennifer Silva Redmond
A Year in Ink, Vol. 4 (2011), edited by Jericho Brown and Laurel Corona
A Year in Ink, Vol. 5 (2012), edited by Brandon Cesmat and T. Greenwood
A Year in Ink, Vol. 6 (2013), edited by Michael Klam and Anthony Bonds

PEN Center USA salutes

A YEAR IN INK
Volume 6

Congratulations!

PEN Center USA is a membership organization that aims
to stimulate and maintain interest in the written word,
to foster a vital literary culture in the western United States,
and to defend freedom of expression
domestically and internationally.

Join the six hundred published authors,
literary community supporters, students, and booksellers
who support our causes today at www.penusa.org.

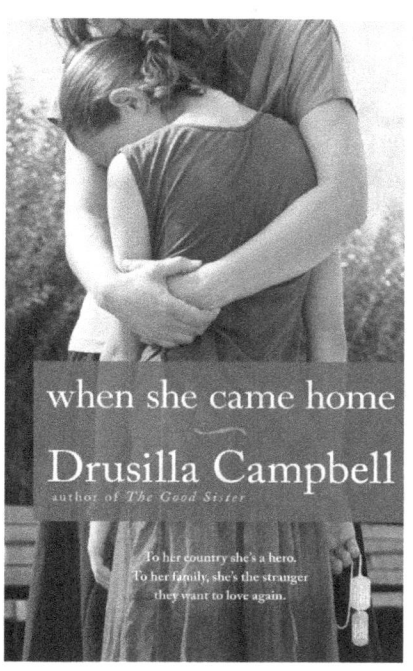
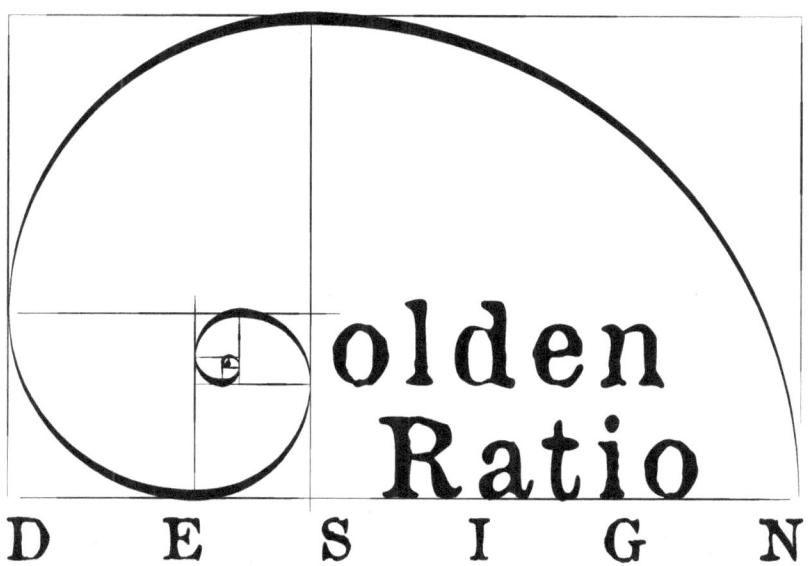

San Diego Writers, Ink
Explore, Discover, Create

CONNECT

THROUGH WRITING

JOIN

- Discounted tuition for workshops and classes
- Reduced submission rates for contests and *A Year in Ink*
- Free use of Room to Write

Individual: $35/year
Household: $50/year
Students/Low-Income: $20/year

ADVERTISE

San Diego Writers, Ink offers three advertising rates for our popular annual anthology *A Year in Ink*.

1/4 page $50   1/2 page $75   Full page $125

Get your business in front of the literary community
(& their family and friends)

contact@sandiegowriters.org for more details

SANDIEGOWRITERS.ORG

www.ingramcontent.com/pod-product-compliance
Lightning Source LLC
Chambersburg PA
CBHW070937250626
47159CB00009B/3283